*A Paddler's Guide to
Eastern North Carolina*

A Paddler's Guide to Eastern North Carolina

**Bob Benner and
Tom McCloud**

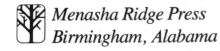
Menasha Ridge Press
Birmingham, Alabama

Library of Congress Cataloging-in-Publication Data

Benner, Bob.
  A paddler's guide to eastern North Carolina

  Includes index.
  1. Canoes and canoeing—North Carolina—Guide-books.
I. McCloud, Tom. II. Title.
GV776.N74B47 1987   917.56   86-31091
ISBN 0-89732-041-7

*Photo Credits: Cover photo of Merchants Mill Pond, pages
152 and 253 by Tom Coffee; all other photos by Bob Benner.*

Menasha Ridge Press
P.O. Box 43673
Birmingham, Alabama 35243
www.menasharidge.com

Contents

Acknowledgments

The authors would like to acknowledge the many people whose assistance made this undertaking possible. There are so many, too numerous to mention individually, who lent a helping hand in one way or another. A few whose efforts require a special note of thanks are:

Donna Benner for her patience with the works in progress and for typing the manuscript.

Allen Trelease for his work on the Ararat, Flat, Reedy Fork, and Snow Creek.

Ralph Steel and Buster Thompson for their notes on Chicod, Contentnea and Tranters creeks, and the Tar River.

Dave Bennie for his help on the Black and South rivers.

Dennis Huntley for his notes on the Uwharrie.

Al Carpenter, Charlie Horton, and Alberta McKay of the State Geological Survey for their cooperation and assistance in using the map library.

Paul Ferguson who was always ready to go.

And last, but certainly not least, all of our friends in the Blue Ridge Canoe Club, Carolina Canoe Club, and North Carolina Outing Club who joined us paddling those swamps, dry creeks, and sometimes-flooded rivers on some of the hottest days of summer as well as during some of the coldest winter rains. After all, what are friends for? We've chased the wild goose and hopefully are the better for it.

Introduction

This guide has been written for the use of the recreational open boater who prefers his cruising type craft to the decked canoes and kayaks. Much of the water included is suitable for novice paddlers; however, some of it will test the skills of the intermediate decked boat paddler. The fact that it is primarily directed toward the open boater should be kept in mind when referring to the rapid classification system used here. It is quite difficult to class a rapid and remain totally objective because that judgment is generally relative to one's experience. In any case, it is hoped that the system will be consistent.

As the sport of canoeing grows, one sees more and more clubs being organized with canoeing as their main interest. Some longtime paddlers question the need for such growth or organization and rightly so, but this is one of the few safe proving grounds available for aspiring canoeists. It is primarily through clubs that one can obtain competent instruction toward improving skills and learning safe canoeing practices. Also, it is only by organization that our free-flowing rivers will be saved for future generations.

Information on safety has been included because of the certain hazards involved in the sport. Hopefully the suggestions made will lessen the possibilities of accidents other than the normal swampings and dunkings that are likely to occur.

Along with these suggestions are rules that will be helpful for the canoeist who decides that Labor Day shouldn't necessarily mean the end of the season. More and more paddlers are venturing forth in the middle of winter to experience a completely different world. The risks increase as the air and water temperature decrease. A familiarity with certain risks relating to exposure can cut down considerably on these inherent risks.

The average canoeist in North Carolina seems to harbor the idea that he has an inalienable right to paddle on any stream that has enough water to float his canoe. This most certainly is a misconception under present interpretation of state law, and an attempt to clarify what the rights of the canoeist may be is discussed.

An explanation of the overall format has been included so that the reader can fully understand the organization of all the information provided on the streams and various sections that this information is divided into. In *Canoeing White Water*, Randy Carter established such an understandable outline in describing rivers that the authors have followed it rather closely.

Finally, the major organization of the book contains seven sections on rivers. Each section consists of streams within one of the seven major river basins located primarily in the Piedmont and Coastal Plains areas of the state.

Unless otherwise indicated, the scale for the maps in this book is a half inch to a mile.

The authors hope the reader finds a small measure of the pleasure they have experienced paddling the miles of white, brown, and black waters contained herein.

PART ONE

Carolina Overview

Physiologically, North and South Carolina are sisters. Both are bordered on the west by the Blue Ridge Mountains and on the east by the Atlantic Ocean. Moving west to east in either state, three major physiologic regions are encountered: the Blue Ridge Mountains, the Piedmont, and the Coastal Plain. In both states the Coastal Plain is locally referred to as "the lowlands," while the Piedmont and Mountain regions are collectively known as the "uplands" or "highlands."

The Blue Ridge Mountains are the eastern part of the Appalachian Mountain System, extending from southeastern Pennsylvania across Maryland, Virginia, North Carolina, South Carolina, and northern Georgia. In North Carolina, the Blue Ridge forms the eastern section of a mountain chain more than 75 miles wide, where cross ridges connect the more westerly Black Mountains and Great Smokies. In this area, known as "the Land of the Sky," are 43 peaks of over 6,000 feet and 125 others of more than 5,000 feet. Mountain valleys here are characteristically narrow, deep, and densely forested, with elevations consistently above 2,000 feet.

By contast, western South Carolina extends only slightly into the Blue Ridge Mountains, where a small number of peaks not exceeding 3,600 feet rise rather abruptly from the foothills. Where mountains occupy approximately 6,000 square miles in North Carolina, there are only about 500 square miles of mountain terrain in South Carolina. The highest point in South Carolina is Sassafrass Mountain (3,560 feet), situated on the North Carolina/South Carolina state line.

The coolest and wettest portion of both states, the Blue Ridge Mountain region is not farmed extensively or densely populated, with the steepness of the terrain making the land more suitable for forest than for farms.

Geologically, the region is underlain by crystalline rocks such as granite, slate, and gneiss, which are dense and hard. The mountains are usually steep with V-shaped valleys. Slopes are covered with thick soil and luxurious forests which retard runoff.

Many rivers are born high in the mountains of the Carolinas, flowing down in all directions like chocolate on a sundae. Typically running along steep, rocky channels, the streams roll swiftly down the mountains over an abundance of rapids and falls, broadening when they reach the valley floors. West of the Blue Ridge the streams flow north and west, forming a major part of the Tennessee River drainage. To the north are the headwaters of the New, which eventually empties into the Ohio. On the southeastern slopes of the Blue Ridge the Broad, Catawba, and Yadkin are born. These merger with other drainages after crossing into South Carolina and finally find their way to the Atlantic Ocean. To the south are the headwaters of the Savannah River, which follows the South Carolina/Georgia border to the sea.

Beyond the Blue Ridge to the east the Carolinas drop out of the mountains and onto the rolling plateau of the Piedmont. Extending from the Blue Ridge escarpment to the fall line where the topography suddenly drops off onto the flat expense of the Coastal Plain, the Piedmont descends at roughly three and a half feet per mile, with the terrain changing gradually from rolling hills to flat upland. Deeply cut by rivers and creeks, the hills of the Piedmont rise from 400 to 1,500 feet above sea level. Though the Piedmont is underlain by the same crystalline rock as the Blue Ridge region, it lacks the mountains' high relief. Only occasionally are the rolling plains punctuated by a prominent hill. Comprising about 40 percent of the area of both Carolinas, the Piedmont is generally well developed and populated. Rivers flowing through the Piedmont, while lacking the high gradient and pristine setting of the mountains, are generally attractive, and some are endowed with a variety of rapids and falls.

The Coastal Plain region of the Carolinas begins at the fall line, where the underlying geology abruptly changes from hard crystalline rock to sandy loam over marl. Known locally as "the low country," the plain was at the bottom of the Atlantic Ocean in the past geologic ages. The fall line, where a dramatic drop in elevation occurs as one moves east from the Piedmont into the Coastal Plain, runs very roughly on the line of Falls-of-the-Roanoke to Durham to Columbia to Augusta, Georgia. Near the fall line the Coastal Plain consists of small hills. Moving toward the ocean, the terrain flattens. Swamp and marsh characterize the coastline corridor to the far east with many natural lakes occurring. Below the mouth of the Cape Fear River the coastal environs assume a more tropical look with black water (caused by tannic acid from decaying vegetation), thick groves of palmettos, magnolias, tall cypress draped with Spanish moss, and live oak.

The Carolinas are alive with beautiful and diverse flora and fauna. Because of their great variety of climate and soil they have the greatest variety of plant life of any area in the eastern United States. Longleaf pine dominates the upper Coastal Plain, along with water oaks and hickories. In the Piedmont, pine remains plentiful, but hardwood forests are the order of the day with deciduous oak being most prevalent, followed by beech, birch, ash, maple, black walnut, sycamore, and yellow popular. On the mountains the forest is generally comprised of oak, chestnut, laurel, white pine, and hemlock. Wildlife is abundant and varied, especially birds, many of which winter and breed in the coastal marshes.

Climate in the Carolinas is equable and pleasant, being cool in the mountains and almost subtropical on the Coastal Plain with the Piedmont representing the middle of the spectrum. Temperatures average approximately ten degrees cooler in the mountains than in the low country. The mean annual temperature for North Carolina is about 59 degrees and for South Carolina 63 degrees, with January being the coldest month and July the warmest. North Carolina receives more rain than South Carolina owing to its larger mountain region. Averages for both states aproximate 54 inches in the mountains, 47 inches in the Piedmont, and 48 inches in the Coastal Plain. On the east slope of some mountains the precipitation is exceptionally heavy. Heavy snow is unusual except in the mountains. Winds are variable and seldom violent except during the storms of fall along the coast.

Clubs and Organizations

There are a number of local and national organizations that the paddler should be aware of. We have attempted to list those groups that we are acquainted with that are active in the surrounding area.

Most local clubs have as their main objectives the training of members toward safer canoeing and the preservation of the streams on which they paddle. Generally they have regularly scheduled trips throughout most of the year and periodically publish newsletters, which are in themselves a valuable source of information for the canoeist.

For those who wish to improve their skills in the canoe, it is almost a necessity to paddle with those of greater experience. In many areas "the local club" will be the only source of such experience.

Many of us begin paddling to get away from the hustle and bustle of today's busy life, to get back to nature, to see things that few others see, or to engage in an activity that few people do. For this reason joining a club and participating in organized trips might seem alien to us. However, the fact remains that without organizations that are willing to work and fight toward preserving our free-flowing streams, there may be none to enjoy in the future. We don't wish to see our rivers become the "L.A. Freeway" at rush hour, but can we afford to be so selfish as to want to keep our favorite streams all to ourselves? How much weight will a handful carry when the Corps begins surveying for the best damsite? Your "bag" may be an occasional quiet float trip down your favorite stream with one or two close friends, but we hope you will see fit to support the organization in your area that may help you save that stream someday. We can save our rivers only if our numbers are large and we are well organized. Not quantity alone, but quantity with quality will be needed. A good source for determining whether or not there is a club in your area might be your canoeing outfitter.

Local and Area

Carolina Canoe Club
P.O. Box 12932
Raleigh, NC 27605-2932

Blue Ridge Canoe Club
P.O. Box 1938
Morganton, NC 28655

Lumber River Canoe Club
P.O. Box 7493
Lumberton, NC 28358

Triangle Paddlers
P.O. Box 20902
Raleigh, NC 27619

Piedmont Paddlers Canoe Club
615 Carolina Avenue
Gastonia, NC 27114

Western Carolina Paddlers
P.O. Box 8541
Asheville, NC 28814

Triad River Runners
P.O. Box 24094
Winston–Salem, NC 27114-4094

National

American Whitewater Affiliation
1430 Fenwick Lane
Silver Springs, MD 20910

Composed of boating clubs and individuals interested in whitewater paddling. It promotes conservation, cruising, and wild water and slalom competitions.

American Canoe Association
7432 Alban Station Boulevard
Suite B-232
Springfield, VA 22150

Comprised of individual members and clubs organized into regional divisions, the ACA conducts cruises; promotes canoe sailing, poling, and sea kayaking; encourages and sanctions competition on all levels; and has conservation as one of its prime areas of interest. *Paddler,* the ACA's official publication, is published monthly.

Conservation Organizations

We are losing our free-flowing rivers and streams one by one in the frantic push for development. Whether that development be by damming, channelization, or dredging, many miles of wild, wonderful water will soon be lost forever. One of our most precious resources is literally going down the drain slowly but surely. We all must stand up and be heard if we are to stem the tide and save some of these waters for our future generations to know and enjoy.

There are many national and local organizations that have as one of their primary objectives the preservation of free-flowing waters. We list only a few of these in hopes the reader might see fit to join in and support the cause.

American Rivers
1025 Vermont Avenue NW
Suite 720
Washington, D.C. 20005

Founded in 1973, the American Rivers publishes a newsletter that contains articles about recent action in Congress dealing with wild and scenic rivers and with water resource projects. Also covered are the progress of wild and scenic river studies being performed by federal agencies and state scenic river programs.

In addition to reporting on current events, the newsletter gives suggestions on how individuals can take action to help protect rivers.

Conservation Council of North Carolina
P.O. Box 12071
Raleigh, NC 27605

The Conservation Council of North Carolina is a statewide organization that coordinates activities of the many conservation groups within North Carolina. A monthly newsletter is published commenting on the various environmental concerns in the state. Among the many special committees of CCNC is the River Preservation Committee.

Sierra Club
85 2nd Street
Second Floor
San Francisco, CA 94105-3441

There are many active chapters of the Sierra Club in North Carolina, most found in the more populous areas of the state. Many of the groups have canoeing activities throughout the year. Since chapter presidents change from year to year, you will need to call the national chapter of the Sierra Club to get the most up-to-date information on whom to contact in your area. Call (415) 977-5500.

National Carolina Natural and Scenic Rivers

The North Carolina General Assembly created a Natural and Scenic Rivers System in 1971, eight years after Congress passed the National Wild and Scenic

Rivers Act. These legislative measures were designed to preserve and protect certain free-flowing rivers in their natural states. A 13-mile segment of the Linville River and some 26.5 miles of the New and the South Fork of the New were the first rivers included in the state's Natural and Scenic Rivers System in 1976. The state tread lightly around the troubled waters of establishing scenic rivers. Opposition, primarily from landowners, met the first designations. A 4.2-mile stretch of the Horsepasture River is currently the shortest scenic river segment in the nation. It entered the system in 1986 after plans for a hydroelectric station threatened to ruin the stream's magnificent scenery. The Lumber River and Wilson Creek are North Carolina's most recent additions to the system, with 81 and 23 designated miles respectively.

State Water Trails

In 1973 a state trails committee was established by the General Assembly to represent the citizens' trail interests. Included are trails for off-the-road vehicles (ORVs), hikers, horseback riders, bicyclists, and canoeists. Today, the state's trails are managed largely by the North Carolina Department of Environment and Natural Resources' Division of Parks and Recreation. Many of the individuals and groups who helped establish the system's trails are still involved in upkeep and publicity locally. In 1978 some 62 miles of the upper Lumber River received recognition as the state's first water trail. A stretch of the French Broad received similar recognition later that year. Since that time, the lower Lumber to the South Carolina border and 165 miles of the Yadkin were included. In addition to these, approximately 1,400 miles of other streams and lakes are deemed to have potential for establishment as water trails.

Many seem to question the need for state water trails. The thinking is that the trail is already there—from highway bridge to highway bridge. A canoe can be dropped in here and floated to there, and a sign marking it as a state water trail isn't going to change that, so why bother?

Perhaps the primary reason for such designation is that a water trail will be identified as a state recreational resource instead of simply a waterway in which to dump one's garbage or effluent to be carried away downstream and out of sight or perhaps a source for a minute amount of hydroelectric power generation. Not that becoming a state water trail will stop such misuse, but the fact that a river has been recognized as a useful and valuable recreational resource may give the stream some protection for future recreational purposes. This is only one step in the process, but it may be one step that was taken in time.

Paddler Information

The most widely publicized of the *paddler* self-evaluations was created by the Keel-Haulers Canoe Club of Ohio. This system brings the problem of matching paddlers with rivers into perspective but seems to overemphasize nonpaddling skills. A canoe clinic student who is athletically inclined but almost totally without paddling skill once achieved a rating of 15 points using the Keel-Haulers system. His rating, based almost exclusively on general fitness and strength, incorrectly implied that he was capable of handling many Class 2 and Class 3 rivers. A second problem evident in the system is the lack of depth in skill category descriptions. Finally, confusion exists in several rating areas as to whether the evaluation applies to open canoes, decked canoes, or both.

To remedy these perceived shortcomings and to bring added objectivity to paddler self-evaluation, Bob Sehlinger* has attempted to refine the paddler rating system. Admittedly the refined system is more complex and exhaustive, but not more so than warranted by the situation. Heavy emphasis is placed on paddling skills, with description adopted from several different evaluation formats, including a nonnumerical system proposed by Dick Schwind.**

Rating the Paddler

The paddler rating system that follows will provide a numerical point summary. The paddler can then use this information to gauge whether a river of a given ranking is within his or her capabilities.

Instructions: All items, except the first, carry points that may be added to obtain an overall rating. All items except "Rolling Ability" apply to both open and decked boats. Rate open and decked boat skills separately.

1. Prerequisite Skills. Before paddling on moving current, the paddler should:
   a. Have some swimming ability.
   b. Be able to paddle instinctively on nonmoving water (lake). (This presumes knowledge of basic strokes.)

---

*Sehlinger, Bob. *A Canoeing and Kayaking Guide to the Streams of Tennessee.* 2 vols. Hillsborough, North Carolina: Menasha Ridge Press, 1983.
**Schwind, Dick. "Rating Systems for Boating Difficulty." *American Whitewater Journal*, vol. 20, no. 3 (May/June 1975).

    c. Be able to guide and control the canoe from either side without changing paddling sides.

    d. Be able to guide and control the canoe (or kayak) while paddling backward.

    e. Be able to move the canoe (or kayak) laterally.

    f. Understand the limitations of the boat.

    g. Be practiced in "wet exit" if in a decked boat.

2. Equipment. Award points on the suitability of your equipment to whitewater. Whether you own, borrow, or rent the equipment makes no difference. *Do not* award points for both *Open Canoe* and *Decked Boat.*

Open Canoe

0 Points	Any canoe less than 15 feet for tandem; any canoe less than 14 feet for solo.
1 Point	Canoe with moderate rocker, full depth, and recurved bow; should be 15 feet or more in length for tandem and 14 feet or more in length for solo and have bow and stern painters.
2 Points	Whitewater canoe. Strong rocker design, full bow with recurve, full depth amidships, no keel; meets or exceeds minimum length requirements as described under "1 Point"; made of hand-laid fiberglass, Kevlar®, Marlex®, or ABS *Royalex®*; has bow and stern painters. Canoe as described under "1 Point" but with extra flotation.
3 Points	Canoe as described under "2 Points" but with extra flotation.

Decked Boat (K-1, K-2, C-1, C-2)

0 Points	Any decked boat lacking full flotation, spray skirt, or foot braces.
1 Point	Any fully equipped decked boat with a wooden frame.
2 Points	Decked boat with full flotation, spray skirt and foot braces; has grab loops; made of hand-laid fiberglass, Marlex®, or Kevlar®.
3 Points	Decked boat with foam wall reinforcement and split flotation; Neoprene® spray skirt; boat has knee braces, foot braces, and grab loops; made of hand-laid fiberglass or Kevlar® only.

3. Experience. Compute the following to determine *preliminary points,* then convert the preliminary points to *final points* according to the conversion table.

Number of days spent each year paddling:

Class I rivers × 1 = _____

Class II rivers × 2 = _____

Class III rivers × 3 = _____

Class IV rivers × 4 = _____

Class V rivers × 5 = _____

Preliminary Points Subtotal _____

Number of years paddling experience × subtotal =

Total Preliminary Points _____

Conversion Table

Preliminary Points	Final Points
0–20	0
21–60	1
61–100	2
101–200	3
201–300	4
301–up	5

Note: This is the only evaluation item where it is possible to accrue more than 3 points.

4. Swimming

0 Points   Cannot swim

1 Point   Weak swimmer

2 Points   Average swimmer

3 Points   Strong swimmer (competition level or skin diver)

5. Stamina

0 Points   Cannot run mile in less than 10 minutes

1 Point   Can run a mile in 7 to 10 minutes

2 Points   Can run a mile in less than 7 minutes

6. Upper-Body Strength

0 Points   Cannot do 15 push-ups

1 Point   Can do 16 to 25 push-ups

2 Points   Can do more than 25 push-ups

7. Boat Control
0 Points Can keep boat fairly straight
1 Point   Can maneuver in moving water; can avoid big obstacles
2 Points Can maneuver in heavy water; knows how to work with the current
3 Points Finesse in boat placement in all types of water; uses current to maximum advantage

8. Aggressiveness
0 Points Does not play or work river at all
1 Point   Timid; plays a little on familiar streams
2 Points Plays a lot; works most rivers hard
3 Points Plays in heavy water with grace and confidence

9. Eddy Turns
0 Points Has difficulty making eddy turns from moderate current
1 Point   Can make eddy turns in either direction from moderate current; can enter moderate current from eddy
2 Points Can catch medium eddies in either direction from heavy current; can enter very swift current from eddy
3 Points Can catch small eddies in heavy current

10. Ferrying
0 Points Cannot ferry
1 Point   Can ferry upstream and downstream in moderate current
2 Points Can ferry upstream in heavy current; can ferry downstream in moderate current
3 Points Can ferry upstream and downstream in heavy current

11. Water Reading
0 Points Often in error
1 Point   Can plan route in short rapid with several well-spaced obstacles
2 Points Can confidently run lead in continuous Class 2; can predict the effects of waves and holes on boat
3 Points Can confidently run lead in continuous Class 3; has knowledge to predict and handle the effects of reversals, side currents, and turning drops.

12. Judgment
0 Points Often in error
1 Point   Has average ability to analyze difficulty of rapids
2 Points Has good ability to analyze difficulty of rapids and make independent judgments as to which should not be run

3 Points   Has the ability to assist fellow paddlers in evaluating the difficulty of rapids; can explain subtleties to paddlers with less experience

13. Bracing
0 Points   Has difficulty bracing in Class 2 rivers
1 Point   Can correctly execute bracing strokes in Class 2 water
2 Points   Can correctly brace in intermittent whitewater with medium waves and vertical drops of 3 feet or less
3 Points   Can brace effectively in continuous whitewater with large waves and large vertical drops (4 feet and up)

14. Rescue Ability
0 Points   Self-rescue in flatwater
1 Point   Self-rescue in mild whitewater
2 Points   Self-rescue in Class 3; can assist others in mild whitewater
3 Points   Can assist others in heavy whitewater

15. Rolling Ability
0 Points   Can only roll in pool
1 Point   Can roll 3 out of 4 times in moving current
2 Points   Can roll 3 out of 4 times in Class 2 whitewater
3 Points   Can roll 4 out of 5 times in Class 3 and 4 whitewater

Add up your points from items 2 through 15. Then compare your score with the "Total Points" in table 2 (page 15) to determine your skill level.

Winter Canoeing

Winter canoeing can be beautiful but it also can be quite dangerous unless certain precautions are taken. Some rules that should be followed by open boaters are:
(1) Exert extreme care in paddling on larger rivers where you cannot walk to shore if a spill occurs. A swim could prove fatal.
(2) Wear a vest-type personal flotation device (PFD) for its additional insulation value. No matter how strong a swimmer you may be, the shock of entering very cold water could prevent you from reaching your PFD.
(3) Always have at least three canoes in the party.
(4) Everyone should have a complete change of clothing in a waterproof container that will withstand pressures of immersion.

Table 1. Rating the River*

Points	Secondary Factors — Factors Related Primarily to Success in Negotiating			Primary Factors — Factors Affecting Both Success & Safety					Secondary Factors — Factors Related Primarily to Safe Rescue		
	Obstacles, rocks, and trees	Waves	Turbulence	Bends	Length (feet)	Gradient (ft./mile)	Resting or Rescue Spot	Water Velocity (mph)	Width and Depth	Temp. °(F)	Accessibility
0	None	Few inches high, avoidable	None	Few, very gradual	<100	<5, regular slope	Almost anywhere	<3	Narrow (<75 ft.) & shallow (<3 ft.)	>65	Road along river
1	Few, passage almost straight through	Low (up to 1 ft.), regular, avoidable	Minor eddies	Many, gradual	100–700	5–15, regular slope		3–6	Wide (>75 ft.) & shallow (<3 ft.)	55–65	<1 hr. travel by foot or water
2	Courses easily recognizable	Low to med. (up to 3 ft.), regular, avoidable	Medium eddies	Few, sharp, blind; scouting necessary	700–5,000	15–40, ledges or steep drops		6–10	Narrow (<75 ft.) & deep (>3 ft.)	45–55	1 hr. to 1 day travel by foot or water
3	Maneuvering course not easily recognizable	Med. to large (up to 5 ft.), mostly regular, avoidable	Strong eddies & crosscurrents		5,000	>40, steep drops, small falls	Good one below every danger spot	>10 or flood	Wide (>75 ft.) & deep (>3 ft.)	<45	>1 day travel by foot or water
4	Intricate maneuvering; course hard to recognize	Large, irregular, avoidable; or med. to large, unavoidable	Very strong eddies, strong crosscurrents								
5	Course tortuous, frequent scouting	Large, irregular, unavoidable	Large-scale eddies & crosscurrents, some up & down								
6	Very tortuous; always scout from shore	Very large (>5 ft.), irregular, unavoidable, special equipment required						Almost none			

SOURCE: Prepared by Guidebook Committee — AWA (from "American White Water," Winter 1957).
*To rate a river, match the characteristics of the river with descriptions in *each* column. Add the points from each column for a total river rating.

Table 2. Ratings Comparisons

International Rating	Approximate Difficulty	Total Points (from Table 1)	Approximate Skill Required
I	Easy	0–7	Practiced Beginner
II	Requires care	8–14	Intermediate
III	Difficult	15–21	Experienced
IV	Very difficult	22–28	Highly Skilled (several with organized group)
V	Exceedingly difficult	29–35	Team of Experts
VI	Utmost difficulty, near limit of navigability		

(5) Each participant should carry on his person a supply of matches in a waterproof container.

(6) Remember that the classification of any particular river is automatically upgraded when canoeing in cold weather. This is due to the extreme effects on the body upon immersion in cold water.

Cold Weather Survival

With more and more paddlers going out in cold weather to engage in their sport, a basic knowledge in cold water and cold weather survival is necessary.

When immersed in water, the loss of heat from the body becomes much more rapid, and survival times without suitable clothing in cold water become very short. For instance, wet clothes lose about 90 percent of their insulating value and can cause heat loss 240 times faster than dry clothing.

The following table gives the approximate survival times of humans immersed in water at various temperatures.

Water Temp (F)	Exhaustion or Unconsciousness	Survival Time
32.5	Less than 15 min.	Less than 15-45 min.
32.5-40	15-30 min.	30-90 min.
40-50	30-60 min.	1-3 hrs.
50-60	1-2 hrs.	1-6 hrs.
60-70	2-7 hrs.	2-40 hrs.
70-80	3-12 hrs.	3 hrs.-indefinite

The greatest change in survival time occurs as the water temperature drops below 50°F.

Swimming in cold water increases the flow of water past the body and pumps heat out of the clothing so that, in spite of heat production, the body loses heat more rapidly. If there is no prospect of getting out of the water immediately, survival time will be longer if one does not swim but relies on his life jacket to hold him up. Better still, assume the HELP position (Heat Escape Lessening Position) in which the knees are tucked close to the chest. This allows one to retain body heat longer. It is, therefore, imperative that a life jacket with adequate flotation be worn. Swim only if there is danger downstream.

Wool, along with waterproof outerwear (rain suit), is highly recommended for cold weather paddling. Wool has the unique ability to provide warmth even when wet and to dry from within, thus wicking moisture away. Even better than wool is the wet suit, which is an absolute necessity for those who paddle decked boats. Also, a wool hat can help tremendously in preserving body heat since a great deal of heat is lost through an unprotected head or neck.

Dry clothing should definitely be carried in a waterproof bag on all winter trips and changed into if one gets wet. Quite often you must insist that the victim change clothing and render assistance in changing because of his lack of coordination. The victim more than likely will be totally unaware of his poor reactions.

Symptoms of exposure occur generally as follows: uncontrollable shivering; vague, slow, slurred speech; memory lapses; slowing of reactions, fumbling hands, and apparent exhaustion. Unconsciousness will follow and then death. The mental effects will be similar to those observed in states of extreme fatigue.

In cases of extreme exposure, build a fire; give the victim a warm drink, if he is able to swallow; strip him and put him into a sleeping bag with another person who is also stripped. *Remember* that the victim must be warmed from an outside heat source since he cannot generate his own body heat. *Do not* give the victim any form of alcohol.

Legal Rights of the Canoeist

In any discussion of the legal rights of canoeists the question of navigability arises. It is generally assumed that if a stream is navigable, one has the legal right to float a canoe on it. Basically this is correct in the state of North Carolina.

However, the question remains as to what constitutes "navigability" under the laws of the state. One old case defined a stream that loggers used to float their timber down as navigable, but it is believed that this case defined a limited type of navigable purpose. The general idea seems to be that if a waterway is suitable as a "highway" of commerce, it is navigable and the public has a right to use it. When a navigable stream crosses an owner's land, the state owns the bottom and the owner cannot legally block use of the stream for navigation or fishing.

In a recent decision, when a landowner attempted to block a waterway, declaring it nonnavigable, the California Court of Appeals determined that the test of navigability is met if the stream is capable of boating for pleasure. In making his decision the judge pointed out that the streams of California are a vital recreational resource of the state. Perhaps this case may set a precedent that will be followed in the future in determining the rights of the canoeist. However, with the strong laws protecting the property rights of the individual owner in North Carolina, this may never be pertinent.

When a person owns land over which a "nonnavigable" stream flows, he owns the land under the stream and has the right to control the surface of the water. For this reason, when canoeing on streams of questionable navigability, it is best to observe one's manners to the fullest. If you must cross private property for any reason, request the owner's permission before doing so. Generally speaking, the landowner will be a reasonable person if approached courteously and respectfully. More often than not, the unreasonable property owner is one whose property rights have been abused in the past.

With the popularity of canoeing growing tremendously, travel on our streams is increasing also. Prime examples of such heavy usage can be found already on the Nantahala and the Chattooga. Be sure that you aren't the proverbial straw that breaks the camel's back by committing some careless act that might cause a landowner along a stream of questionable navigability to block access to it, or perhaps to take the next guy to court for trespass. Make sure that you leave the door open for the next guy.

Safety

A section on safety has been included because of the great interest in whitewater canoeing and rafting among the uninitiated. The fact is, there are potential hazards involved in the sport which in many instances is the very reason many are attracted to it. However, with normal precautions and good judgment in determining one's level of skill, it can be a safe sport under normal conditions.

A few tips for the paddler to follow to insure that his trip is an enjoyable one and, above all, a safe one are listed. If each and every one of these rules is followed while on the river, you won't become the proverbial "accident looking for a place to happen."

1. **Never boat alone.** Three boats are generally considered a minimum on anything but small low-water streams.
2. **Always carry a life jacket.** Wear it unless you are a capable swimmer and even then have it on when in water difficult enough that an upset is possible.
3. **Know your ability and don't attempt water beyond this ability.** In considering whether or not to run a particular rapid ask:
   a. Is it much greater in difficulty than anything I've attempted before?
   b. If I try it and don't make it, will I place others in a difficult or dangerous situation in order to rescue me or my boat? If the answer to either one is yes, don't try it. No experienced paddler will ever accuse you of being "chicken" when you back off, but he will respect your good judgment.
4. **Be adequately equipped.** Have an extra paddle in the canoe, if not an extra one for each paddler. Have bow and stern lines 8-15 feet long tied on securely to the ends of the craft. *Never* tie the ends of these lines in the boat. At the same time, be sure no lines are positioned so that they might entangle the canoeist's feet. The authors once observed a canoe swamp in Nantahala Falls which in itself was

certainly not too unusual nor was it very dangerous. But the paddler came in for what was a terrifying moment when he came up wearing his bailer line around his neck—with the other end still tied to the boat. He simply had far too much line tied to his bailer.

A good standard first-aid kit should be carried in a waterproof container, and a throw line at least 3/8 inches in size, 75-100 feet long, preferably polypropylene, can become a necessity on all except the small shallow streams.

5. **If traveling with a group (or club), know the plans of the group, the organization of the trip, and follow the decisions of the leader.** Most clubs have standard trip rules established which determine the trip leader's responsibilities as well as those of each paddler individually.

   One rule generally followed on the river is that each canoe is responsible for keeping the canoe following in sight. This same rule should apply when a caravan of cars is traveling to or from the put-in or take-out.

6. **Scout unfamiliar rapids before running them.** Even those that are familiar can change considerably at different water levels.

7. **Stay off flooded streams.** The great increase in drownings from canoeing and rafting accidents has resulted almost entirely from mishaps on swollen rivers.

8. **Do not attempt to run dams or abrupt ledges.** Quite often a hydraulic jump is formed in which the surface water flows back upstream, causing a rolling action. This rolling action tends to hold a boat or a person in, tumbling them around and around. The only escape is to swim out the end or dive toward the bottom into the downstream current.

9. **If you spill, get to the upstream end of the boat and, if possible, stay with it.** Don't risk the possibility of being pinned against a rock. If others spill, rescue the boaters and then go after the boat and the equipment.

10. **If you get broadside on a rock or other obstacle, lean toward the obstacle—downstream from the direction of the current.** It is the unnatural reaction but the correct thing to do in order to prevent the upstream gunwale from dipping into the current and swamping the boat.

In running smaller low-water streams, the possibility of personal danger is usually not as great as in large-volume rivers, but there are many things to watch for that might prove dangerous if not approached with caution. Some of the most common things that the paddler needs to beware of are logs and trees blocking the passage, barbwire fences which can prove difficult to see, and low-water bridges which may be just high enough to lure the unwary paddler into attempting a run under them. If in doubt when approaching the latter, pull to shore well above it and check out the clearance. The American Whitewater Affiliation has a safety code which is quite inclusive and the aspiring boater should become familiar with it.

River Etiquette

Be considerate of other drivers when unloading boats. Pull off the road as far as possible and do not block the roadway with boats or bodies. We tend to think that no one will mind slowing down or even stopping for a second or two, but this scenario might occur day after day during the peak of the season on a popular stream. The same guy may be caught more than once and soon he will think of all canoeists as inconsiderate SOBs. He may even turn out to be the landowner whose property you might like to camp on. How much luck do you think you will have with your request then?

Be sure you request permission before trespassing, whether putting in, taking out, or camping on private property.

When passing fishermen on the bank or in the stream, steer as clear as possible. Slowing down and paddling as quietly as you can will show that you are trying to be helpful. Remember, there are more of them than us, and they have a much longer reach.

Do not annoy cows or other farm animals that may appear along the banks. The next guy and everyone behind him will get the blame for the sour milk.

Camping Manners

In order to preserve for future generations the qualities of wilderness that we find today, we must try to minimize our impact on such areas as much as possible. We should attempt to leave no visible signs of our visit. There can be a great deal of satisfaction and personal achievement in knowing one has camped in an area without leaving any perceptible trace.

Some suggestions that may prove helpful in accomplishing "no trace" camping follow.

Campsites

Select sites that have natural drainage, thereby avoiding a need for trenching. Never cut boughs or poles unless for an emergency. Minimize building for kitchen emplacements or bed sites. When breaking camp, erase all evidence of having been there.

Fires

Use existing fire sites whenever possible. If camping where no one has camped before, build a small fireplace--away from trees. Clear a wide circle around the site. Above all, do not leave a fire unattended. When breaking camp, drown the fire completely, stir, and drown again until the ashes are cold to touch. Unless in a well-used camp, bury the ashes and return the fireplace rocks to a natural position. Cover all traces.

Wood

Build an "Indian fire," not a "white man's fire." Indian says that white man builds big fire and has to sit far back from it, while Indian builds small fire and sits close in. Keep it small. Use down wood only; do not cut living trees.

Sanitation

Go well away from the water, as well as the campsite, and dig a shallow six-to-eight-inch "cat hole" and bury. Wastes at this level will biodegrade faster than if buried deeper. Do not leave toilet paper strewn about. Such "tulips" are not attractive. Use white paper.

Washing

Do all bathing, clothes washing, and pot scrubbing well back from shore. Prevent pollution by keeping soap and detergent out of all waters. If bathing, rinse on shore before a final dip.

Cleanup and Garbage

Do not bury garbage. Animals and the elements quite often expose it. Carry out everything that will not burn. Many packages are lined with foil and foil will not burn, so check all packages before placing them in the fire. Cans can easily be carried if both ends are cut out and the cans washed or burned and then flattened. Check for litter. Leave your campsite cleaner than you found it.

Courtesy

Do not crowd other sites. Noise is not in harmony with the wilderness. If a radio is a must, keep in mind that it is for your entertainment, not everyone else's. If others do not have radios, assume they don't have them for a reason and therefore would rather not hear one--theirs or yours. Be considerate of others.

Make every trip a clean-up trip! Take nothing but pictures; leave nothing but ripples.

Some Helpful Hints

In smaller streams, check out overhanging branches for snakes.

Those shiny green leaves hanging in abundance over and into the water quite possibly may be poison ivy. Learn to recognize it before you learn that you are allergic.

On larger rivers, be sure to allow for the effects of head winds (are there any other kind?) on your progress when estimating trip times.

If entering tidal waters, check for schedules. Use the outgoing tide to your advantage.

When paddling in swamps or coastal waters, take an adequate amount of insect repellent.

No matter how warm, a long-sleeve shirt, long pants, and a cap for protection from the sun should be considered necessities.

Do not assume water from springs or streams is pure. Use some method of purifying it before drinking. The "green apple quickstep" is not the most enjoyable dance to practice in the "boonies."

A little pre-trip conditioning can help make your trip more enjoyable and, at the same time, provide that little extra in case of an emergency. Paddling under normal conditions requires not so much strength as endurance, so a little aerobic-type activity, such as running or rope jumping, can be good. For the shoulders, back, and arms, push-ups and pull-ups are effective. Start with a few and increase slowly up to, say, eight to ten pull-ups and three sets of ten push-ups. Be sure to go all the way to the floor on the push-ups and to a full arm extension on the pull-ups. For the abdominals, which do come into play while paddling, try bent-knee curl-ups. Lay flat on the back with knees bent and feet unsupported. Cross hands across the chest and grasp opposite shoulders. Suck the gut in and, while exhaling, roll the shoulders off the floor. Work up to three sets of ten. Repeating this routine a minimum of three days a week will make for a far more enjoyable experience.

How to Use This Guide

Description

A brief description of the stream as a whole or of the particular section is given.

Topographic Maps

"Topo Maps" are listed in the order in which the river flows. Unless otherwise noted, all maps are located in the USGS North Carolina Index. If there is not a local source for maps, they are available on order from:

> Branch of Distribution
> U.S. Geological Survey
> Box 25286
> Denver Federal Center
> Denver, CO 80225

Counties

Each stream will have the county in which a particular section is located, and where it flows through more than one, the counties will be listed in the order in which it flows.

Put-In

The exact put-in is listed, such as a particular highway or secondary road bridge. When more than one section is listed, the put-in for the following section will be the take-out for the preceding section.

Drop

The total gradient of a section has been given rather than breaking it down into an average number of feet per mile. This has been done because quite often on a long stretch the gradient might be rather great in one portion and not in another. Where the drop is quite rapid, it will be listed as (1 @ 40') which indicates one mile in the section will drop at the rate of 40 feet within that mile.

Table 3. International Scale for Grading the Difficulty of River Cruising Routes

Rating	River or Individual Rapids Characteristics	Approximate Minimum Experience Required
Smooth Water		
A	Pools, lakes, rivers with velocity under 2 m.p.h.	Beginner
B	Rivers, velocity 2–4 m.p.h.	Beginner with river instructions
C	Rivers, velocity above 4 m.p.h. (max. back-paddling speed). May have some sharp bends or obstructions.	Instructed and practiced beginner
Whitewater		
1	Easy – sand banks, bends without difficulty, occasional small rapids with low regular waves. Correct course may be easy to find but care is needed with minor obstacles like pebble banks, fallen trees, etc., especially on narrow rivers. River speed less than hard back-paddling speed.	Practiced beginner
2	Medium – fairly frequent but unobstructed rapids, usually with regular waves, easy eddies, and easy bends. Course generally easy to recognize. River speeds occasionally exceeding hard back-paddling speed.	Intermediate
3	Difficult – maneuvering in rapids necessary. Small falls, large irregular waves covering boat, numerous rapids. Main current may swing under bushes, branches, or overhangs. Course not always easily recognizable. Current speed usually less than fast forward-paddling speed.	Experienced
4	Very difficult – long extended stretches of rapids, high irregular waves with boulders directly in current. Difficult broken water, eddies, and abrupt bends. Course often difficult to recognize and inspection from the bank frequently necessary. Swift current. Rough water experience indispensable.	Highly skilled (several years experience with organized group)
5	Exceedingly difficult – long rocky rapids with difficult and competely irregular broken water which must be run head-on. Very fast eddies, abrupt bends, and vigorous crosscurrents. Difficult landings increase hazard. Frequent inspections necessary. Extensive experience necessary.	Team of experts
6	Limit of navigability – all previously mentioned difficulties increased to the limit. Only negotiable at favorable water levels. Cannot be attempted without risk of life.	Team of experts

Difficulty

This refers to the rating of difficulty of the rapids located within the particular section of the stream. The rating system used is based on that of the International Scale for Grading the Difficulty of River Cruising Routes, table 3.

It is important to know the difficulty rating of a particular river before setting out on it. The ratings used here are based on normal or ideal water heights. The ratings will vary somewhat as the water level in the stream fluctuates.

The authors have attempted to be as objective as possible in declaring whether a rapid is Class 3 or 4. Such a judgment will vary considerably from person to person according to skill or experience.

Where a section has only one rapid of a higher difficulty than others, it is listed 2-3/4, with the final number representing the one more difficult rapid as a Class 4.

Distance

Measured in miles from county and USGS maps and generally rounded off.

Time

This is actual paddling time on the river, including time for scouting when necessary. When paddling with a group larger than two or three canoes and when a lunch stop will be made, additional time should be planned for.

Scenery

AA   Unusually beautiful even to the spectacular, generally remote and wild.
A   Generally remote and wild. Perhaps some signs of civilization but mostly uninhabited.
B   More pastoral type of country with more settled areas.
C   Fair amount of development, general signs of civilization such as garbage dumps, autos left on the side of the stream, visual pollution.

Water Quality

Excellent   Watershed is protected and water generally remains "clear as crystal."
Good   Some small amount of sediment appears but on the whole the water would be considered clean.
Fair   Heavier sediment in stream but no evident pollution.
Poor   Signs of human or industrial pollution to the extent water is actually discolored.

Gauge

Where there is a USGS gauge located close enough to the put-in or take-out on a particular section, readings have been taken from it. Exceptions are those streams that have enough water volume to be floatable year round; then a gauge reading is not considered necessary.

Whenever possible, a minimum level for solo paddling has been established. Generally a reading of 0.20, or two-tenths of a foot, above that listed for solo will be enough for tandem paddling. (Example: 1.54 minimum solo level; 1.74 for tandem.)

Numerals — 6"
Spaces — 6"

Surface ∿∿∿∿∿∿∿∿∿∿∿∿∿∿∿∿∿ Water Level

Gauge Illustration
Example of Minimum Water Level

On streams where a high level can be extremely dangerous, a maximum reading is given whenever one has been established. Otherwise, water flowing through trees will always be an indicator of questionably high-water conditions.

Where no USGS gauge is available, gauges quite often have been painted, usually on a bridge, at a put-in or take-out. Generally a level of six inches (6") below zero (0) can be considered a minimum for solo paddling.

Difficulties

A brief description of specific points that might present problems for the paddler are listed, hopefully in enough detail that the paddler recognizes them, but not so much that the thrill of running a new river or a particular rapid is taken away.

Directions

In a few sections, detailed directions have been given to a particular put-in or take-out, but in general the maps should prove adequate for locating these points. In the event one wishes to have complete maps of particular counties, they are available from the local county office of the State Highway Engineer or from:

NC Department of Transportation
Location and Surveys Unit
P.O. Box 25201
Raleigh, NC 27611

Where a river flows through several counties, reference will initially be made to a county route by name and number (e.g., Wilkes County Rt. 1509). Thereafter only the route number will be referred to until another road in the next county is introduced.

The authors will appreciate any pertinent comments, corrections, or suggestions that might prove valuable in any future editions.

PART TWO

1

Yadkin–Pee Dee Basin

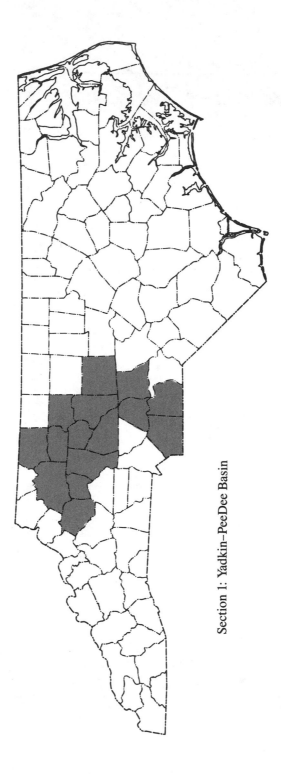

Section 1: Yadkin–PeeDee Basin

Ararat River

The Ararat River is a southward-flowing tributary of the Yadkin. It originates along the Blue Ridge in Virginia and passes through Mt. Airy and along the west side of Pilot Mountain. Compared with Fisher, Mitchell, and other neighboring streams of comparable size, the Ararat seems to keep its water level relatively well in dry spells. This may be attributable in part to its service as the receptacle of Mt. Airy's sewage system. A smell (comparable to that of the Haw) is occasionally noticeable for several miles below town, but water quality has much improved in the past year or two. Unfortunately, there are many evidences of refuse dumping along the upper stretches where the stream gradient is greatest. The second section, by contrast, is a beautiful run, almost totally untouched and isolated.

Topo Maps: Mt. Airy South, Siloam

County: Surry

(1) End of Surry County Rt. 1772, just south of Mt. Airy, to the Rt. 2044 bridge

Drop: 110′
Difficulty: 1-2
Distance: 12.7 mi.

Time: 4.5 hrs.
Scenery: A-B
Water Quality: Fair

Gauge: A USGS gauge is just above the Rt. 2019 bridge at Ararat, on the west bank. Minimum level for solo is 1.20.

Difficulties: Nothing major. An old wooden dam about two miles below the put-in can be run on the right at most water levels, involving a drop of about two feet. There are some ledges of comparable drop farther on. Just above the take-out, a dynamited power dam (no longer recognizable as such) creates a strong Class II rapid.

(2) Surry County Rt. 2044 bridge to Rt. 2080 bridge

Drop: 55′
Difficulty: 1-2
Distance: 8.8 mi.

Time: 3 hrs.
Scenery: A
Water Quality: Fair-Good

Difficulties: None.

The first section may be shortened to nine miles by taking out just above Rt. 2019 bridge at the community of Ararat, on the left bank. The second section can be lengthened by putting in at that point or at NC 268 bridge, less than a mile above the destroyed power dam. NC 268 is a less desirable put-in or take-out than Rts. 2019 upstream and 2044 downstream.

The last four miles of the river, before its confluence with the Yadkin, have a total drop of only ten feet; moreover, there is no convenient take-out downstream on the Yadkin. Those so inclined can paddle up the Yadkin for nine-tenths of a mile to the bridge at Siloam.

Gravel bar along the Yadkin River

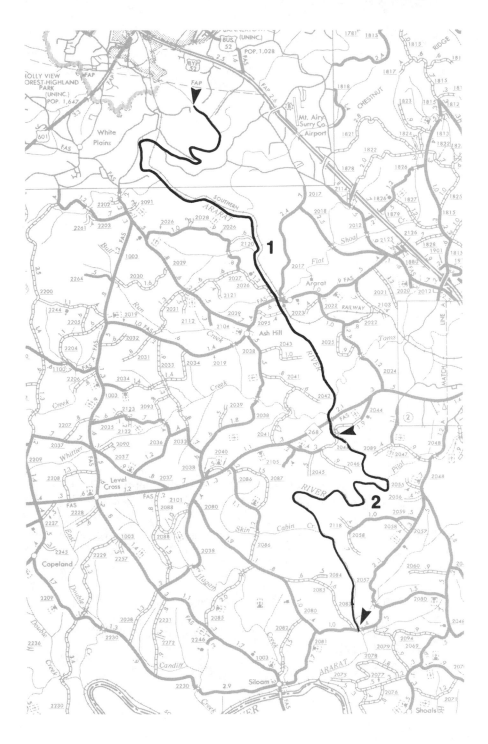

Rocky River

The source of the Rocky River lies southeast of Mooresville in Iredell County, where it begins its flow south and then southeast across Cabarrus County. We pick it up after it enters Stanly and Union counties where it turns east and breaks through the fall line. The sections described are by far the more attractive of those that are runnable.

Topo Maps: Midland, Stanfield, Oakboro, Aquadale, Mt. Gilead, West

Counties: Stanly, Union, Anson

(1) Stanly County Rt. 1140 bridge to NC 200 bridge

Drop: 78'   **Time:** 3 hrs.
Difficulty: 1-2   **Scenery:** A-B
Distance: 6.3 mi.   **Water Quality:** Good

Gauge: Located on north side of Rt. 1140 bridge. Minimum for solo is 3" above the bottom of -1 (below 0).

Difficulties: None, other than many small ledges and extensive rock gardens.

(2) NC 200 bridge to NC 742 bridge

Drop: 46'   **Time:** 3 hrs.
Difficulty: 1-2+   **Scenery:** A
Distance: 7.5 mi.   **Water Quality:** Good

Gauge: Located on north side of NC 200 bridge. Minimum for solo is 3" above the bottom of -1 (below 0).

Difficulties: None, until a big ledge about 200 yards above the take-out. It drops about 6 feet in 25 yards. At higher water levels it might be wise to scout.

(3) NC 742 bridge to NC 138 bridge over Long Creek.

Drop: 37'   **Time:** 2 hrs.
Difficulty: 1-2   **Scenery:** A
Distance: 4.7 mi.   **Water Quality:** Good

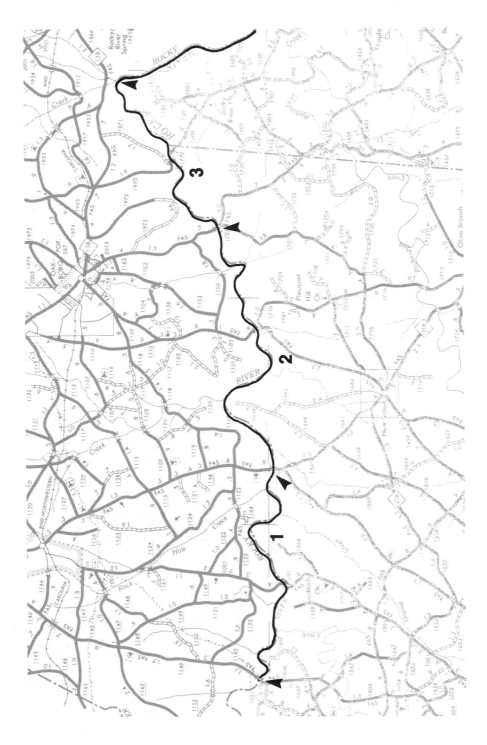

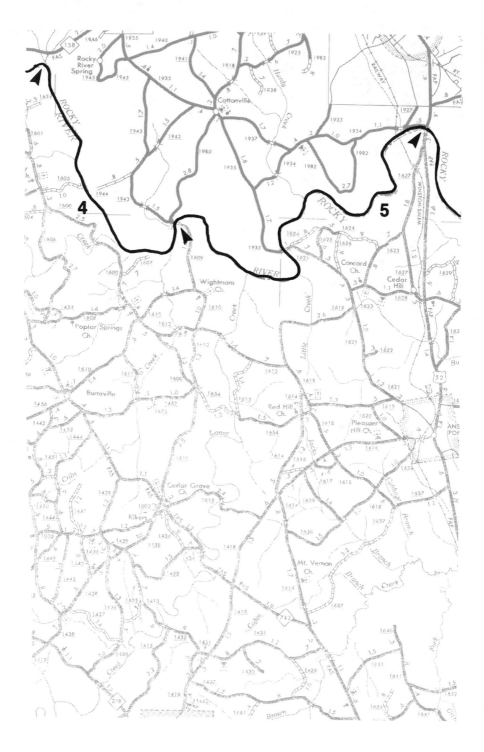

Gauge: Located on north side of NC 742 bridge. Minimum for solo is 3" above the bottom of -1 (below 0).

Difficulties: None, except an occasional ledge.

Note: To reach the take-out, paddle up Long Creek about 150 yards to NC 138 bridge.

(4) NC 138 bridge over Long Creek to Stanly County Rt. 1943 bridge

Drop: 42′
Difficulty: 1-2
Distance: 6.2 mi.

Time: 3 hrs.
Scenery: A
Water Quality: Good

Gauge: See section 3.

Difficulties: There are many ledges and rock gardens which require a great deal of maneuvering at lower water levels.

(5) Stanly County Rt. 1943 to US 52 bridge

Drop: 23′
Difficulty: B-1
Distance: 10.3 mi.

Time: 4 hrs.
Scenery: A-B
Water Quality: Good

Gauge: Runnable year round except during extremely dry conditions.

Difficulties: None.

(6) US 52 bridge to NC 109 wildlife access area on the Pee Dee River

Drop: 16′
Difficulty: B-1
Distance: 11.4 mi.

Time: 4.5 hrs.
Scenery: A-B
Water Quality: Good

Gauge: Runnable year round except during extremely dry season. If Norwood Dam isn't generating the current in the Pee Dee, the four and a half miles downstream can be quite slow and paddling time will undoubtedly be increased.

Difficulties: None.

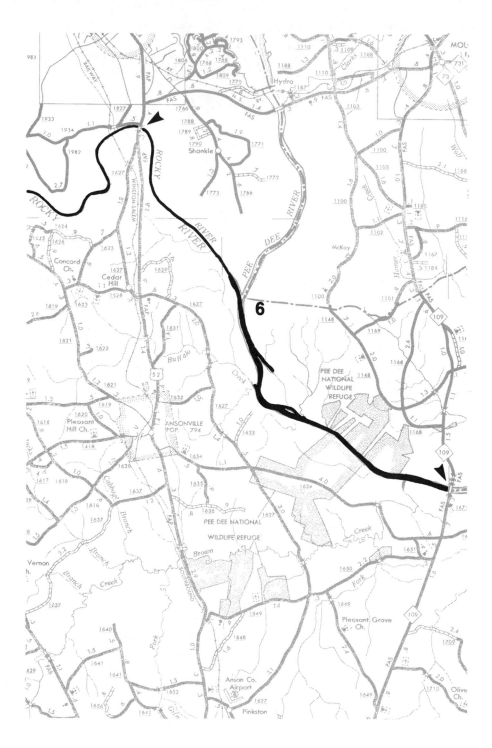

South Yadkin River

The South Yadkin River heads up on the southern slopes of the Brushy Mountains. It flows by Rocky Face (elevation 1,814 feet), the last prominent peak of the Brushy chain, and heads south and east across the Piedmont to join the Yadkin. We pick it up, just southeast of Rocky Face, as it makes its last drop into the more gently rolling hills of the upper plateau.

Sections 6-9 provide some 42 miles of waters suitable for canoe camping.

Note: As streams cut their way through the softer hills of the Piedmont, one will encounter more downed trees, a result of the eroding banks. This becomes the most common difficulty encountered below section 1 and should not be taken lightly--especially at higher water levels.

Topo Maps: Hiddenite, Central, Harmony, Calahaln, Cool Springs, Cooleemee, Churchland

Counties: Alexander, Iredell, Davie, Rowan

(1) Alexander County Rt. 1461 bridge to Rt. 1456 bridge

Drop: 118′	**Time:** 3.5 hrs.
Difficulty: 1-2	**Scenery:** A
Distance: 5 mi.	**Water Quality:** Good

Gauge: On Rt. 1461 bridge on the southeast corner. Reading of 6" below 0 is the minimum for a solo run.

Difficulties: A 12-foot combination dam and ledge is located about 50 yards down from the put-in. Carry on the right. About one mile down, a large tree blocks the only chute. Approach it carefully. About a half mile below the culvert under Rt. 1491, there is an eight-foot ledge, which possibly could be run off center, angling to the right. Farther down, there is a three-foot ledge. Carry on the left.

(2) Alexander County Rt. 1456 bridge to Iredell County Rt. 1561 bridge

Drop: 53′	**Time:** 2.75 hrs.
Difficulty: 1	**Scenery:** A
Distance: 6.8 mi.	**Water Quality:** Good-Fair

Gauge: On Iredell Co. Rt. 1570 bridge on the southeast corner. Reading of 6" below 0 is minimum for solo.

Difficulties: Just below the put-in, a water intake unit at the lower end of the Col. R. L. Tatum Water Plant should be approached cautiously. At slightly higher than normal levels, there are a number of downed trees that could be dangerous.

(3) Iredell County Rt. 1561 bridge to NC 115 bridge

Drop: 29′   **Time:** 3 hrs.
Difficulty: 1   **Scenery:** B
Distance: 4.9 mi.   **Water Quality:** Fair

Gauge: 6" below 0 for minimum.

Difficulties: Many downed trees must be hauled over. A partially washed-out dam about four miles downstream might look tempting. Don't be misled, however, because there are steel reinforcing rods at the bottom of the chute. Carry it on the right. A drive across the bridge above the dam looks as if it would prove as hairy as trying the chute.

(4) NC 115 bridge to Iredell County Rt. 1892 bridge

Drop: 19′   **Time:** 1.5 hrs.
Difficulty: C   **Scenery:** B
Distance: 4.5 mi.   **Water Quality:** Fair

Gauge: 6" below 0. The river from this point downstream would very seldom be too low to run, except during an extremely dry spell.

Difficulties: A few downed trees. An eight-foot slanting dam just above the 1892 bridge. Easy take-out or carry on the right, above the water treatment plant. This is a situation that might lure the neophyte into putting a little excitement into his life. If so, the very heavy hydraulic below won't allow him the opportunity to tell about it.

(5) Iredell County Rt. 1892 bridge to Rt. 2156 bridge

Drop: 19′   **Time:** 2.5 hrs.
Difficulty: C   **Scenery:** A-B
Distance: 7 mi.   **Water Quality:** Fair

Gauge: See section 4.

Difficulties: Heavily clogged up below the US 21 bridge for a short distance.

(6) Iredell County Rt. 2156 bridge to the side of Rt. 2145 (beneath I-40 bridge)

Drop: 28′
Difficulty: C
Distance: 11.3 mi.

Time: 3.5 hrs.
Scenery: A-B
Water Quality: Fair

Gauge: See section 4.

Difficulties: None. Perhaps an occasional downed tree.

(7) Iredell County Rt. 2145 (beneath I-40 bridge) to Rowan County Rt. 1983 bridge

Drop: 21′
Difficulty: C
Distance: 9.2 mi.

Time: 3 hrs.
Scenery: A-B
Water Quality: Fair

Gauge: See section 4.

Difficulties: Watch for possible downed trees.

(8) Rowan County Rt. 1983 bridge to US 601 bridge

Drop: 34′
Difficulty: -1/2
Distance: 11.7 mi.

Time: 3.75 hrs.
Scenery: A-B
Water Quality: Fair

Gauge: See section 4.

Difficulties: Dam at Cooleemee (seven miles below the put-in). Approach it carefully on the right. Take-out is about 30 yards above the dam in a low open area. A well-defined trail leads around the dam, a carry of about 100 yards. A Class 2 chute in the center below is runnable by approaching it from the right.
For those who don't wish to run the two and a half miles of slack water above the dam, a take-out can be made at a ramp at Bear Creek, off Davie County Rt. 1116.

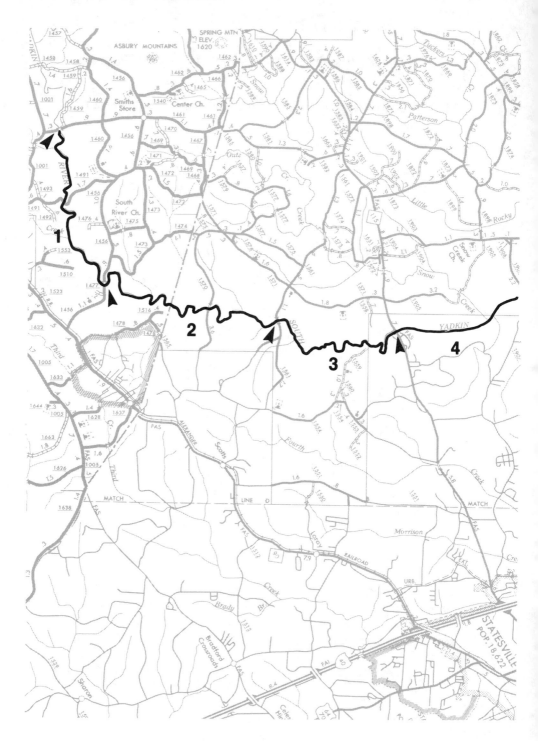

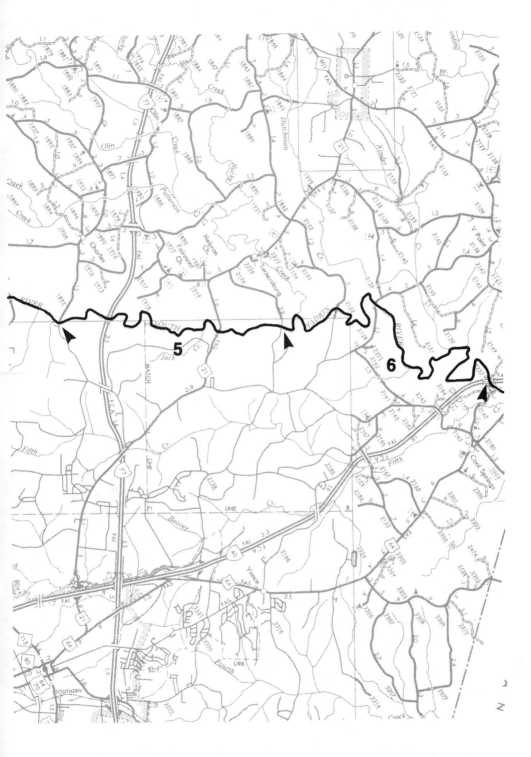

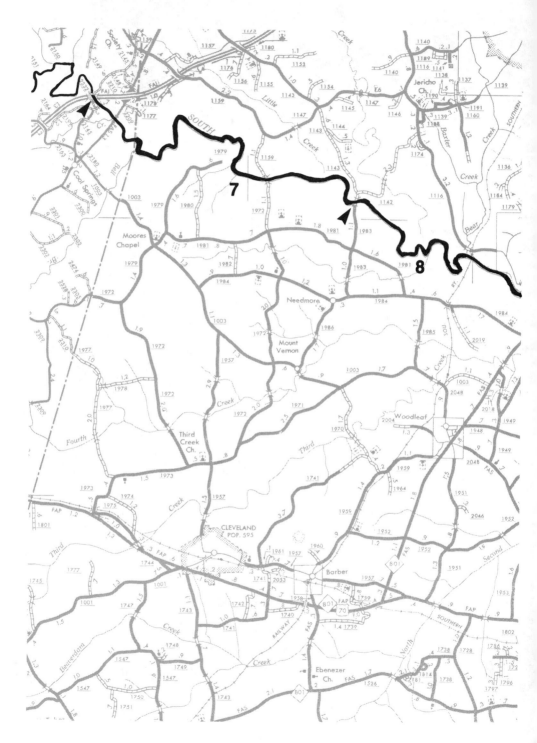

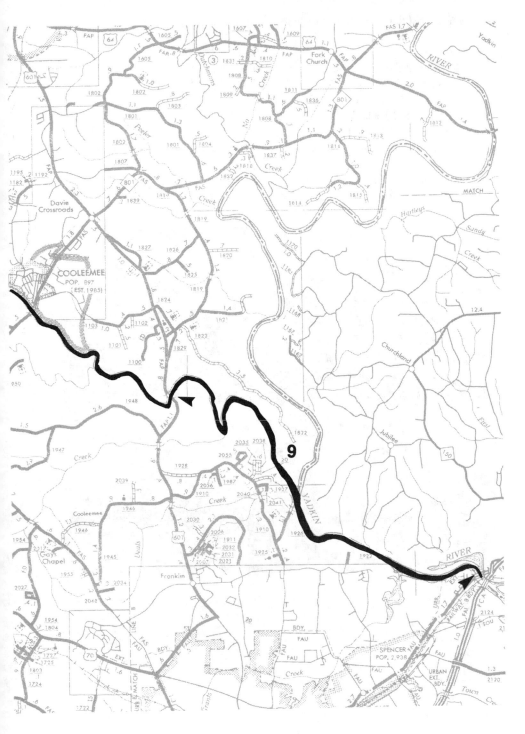

(9) US 601 bridge to NC 150 bridge over the Yadkin River

Drop: 5′
Difficulty: C
Distance: 9.9 mi.

Time: 3 hrs.
Scenery: A-B
Water Quality: Fair

Gauge: See section 4.

Difficulties: None, except maneuvering around an occasional downed tree.

Directions: *Put-in*--North on Alexander County Rt. 1001 off NC 90 in Hiddenite, then east on Rt. 1461. *Take-out*--NC 150 north of Salisbury.

Rocky River

Uwharrie River

The Uwharrie River heads up west of Asheboro and flows generally south through the Uwharrie Mountains and across portions of the Uwharrie National Forest before it flows into Lake Tillery. The river meanders greatly through small floodplains and steep valley walls, which present some very scenic bluffs. The bed is primarily one of long pools with occasional ripples.

The area is widely known for its gold-mining activity. North Carolina's first deep gold mines were found in Montgomery County in the early 1820s. In fact, several mines were worked along the river itself late in the nineteenth century. The largest of these was the Coggins Mine, just up Rt. 1301, west of the river. This was the most important mine in the state from 1915 until the late 1920s. The paddler may want to bring along a pan and take a longer than usual lunch break. It may pay for the gas to run the shuttle--one way, that is!

Note to hikers: A hiking trail, referred to as GUMPAC, has been developed in a corridor along the ridges paralleling the river. The trail, developed primarily through the efforts of a group of private citizens (Greater Uwharrie Mountains Preservation and Appreciation Committee), hopefully will be included soon as a component of the State Trails System.

Topo Maps: Asheboro, Albemarle

Counties: Randolph, Montgomery

(1) NC 49 bridge to Randolph County Rt. 1143 bridge

Drop: 22′	**Time:** 4 hrs.
Difficulty: C-1	**Scenery:** A-B
Distance: 11.5 mi.	**Water Quality:** Fair

Gauge: USGS gauge 100 yards downstream from NC 109 on the north bank. Minimum for solo is 1.6. Runnable year round except during extremely long dry periods.

Difficulties: Watch for an occasional downed tree. A five-foot dam located just above Rt. 1143 bridge can be carried fairly easily on the left side. Approach cautiously at higher water levels. Some two miles of backwater will be found above it.

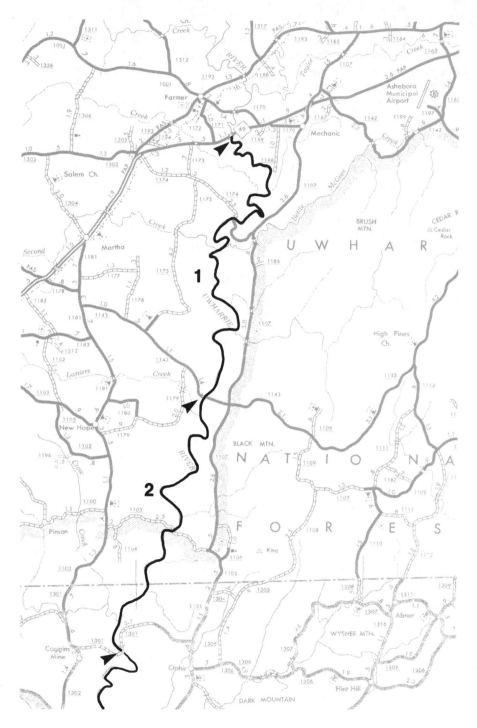

(2) Randolph County Rt. 1143 bridge to Montgomery County Rt. 1301 bridge

Drop: 24'
Difficulty: 1-2
Distance: 7.7 mi.

Time: 2.75 hrs.
Scenery: A
Water Quality: Fair

Gauge: See section 1.

Difficulties: None.

(3) Montgomery County Rt. 1301 bridge to side of Forest Service Rd. 555 (Cotton Place Road), 2.9 miles below NC 109 bridge

Drop: 46'
Difficulty: 1-2
Distance: 10.6 mi.

Time: 4.5 hrs.
Scenery: A
Water Quality: Fair

Gauge: See section 1.

Difficulties: None.

(4) Forest Service Rd. 555 (Cotton Place Road), 2.9 miles below NC 109 bridge, to Morrow Mountain State Park, directly across Lake Tillery from the mouth of the Uwharrie

Drop: 23'
Difficulty: 1-2
Distance: 6.6 mi.

Time: 2.75 hrs.
Scenery: A
Water Quality: Fair

Gauge: See section 1.

Difficulties: None.

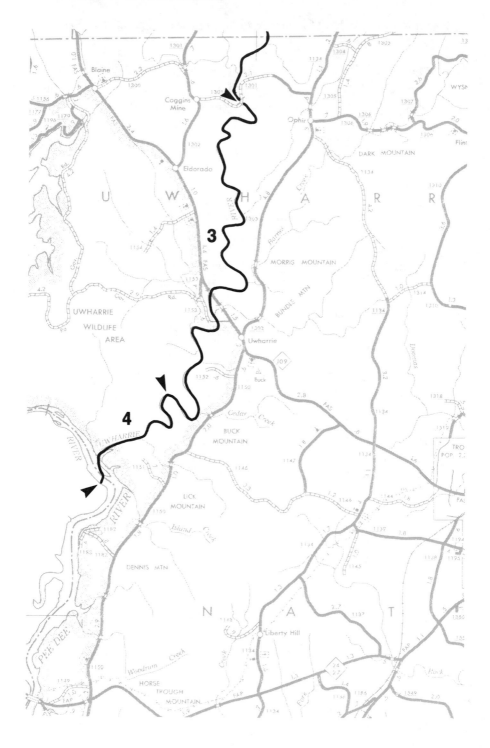

Yadkin River

The Yadkin River heads up in the mountain resort town of Blowing Rock and flows through a remote mountainous area of Caldwell County before coming alongside US 321 about three miles north of Patterson. It moves generally northeasterly through "Happy Valley" into Kerr Scott Lake and then meanders through five counties before entering the impoundment at High Rock Lake in Davidson County. Two additional impoundments, Badin and Tillery, follow immediately, after which the Yadkin becomes the Pee Dee and flows into South Carolina.

The river is primarily pastoral down from Patterson, moving over occasional low ledges and through shallow rock gardens. Below Kerr Scott Dam it continues on much the same, although considerably wider and with fewer rapids, until it makes the big bend to the south below Siloam. Here, it drops fairly fast for a couple of miles over a series of shoals, which can become formidable in medium-high waters.

The one other point of difficulty on the river is Idols Dam, which is downstream from I-40 bridge and just below Tanglewood Park. Water flows over the dam and it should be approached with great caution.

Naturally, a waterway crossing as much of a state as the Yadkin does carries with it much history--in fact, too much to delve into here in any detail. However, in section 3 it is of interest to note that the Daniel Boone family had two homesites in the vicinity in the 1760s. The first was near Beaver Creek, about three-quarters of a mile south of the river, where the hearth still stands; the second was on the north side of the river just below the mouth of Beaver Creek. It was from here that Boone left on his trek to Kentucky in April 1775.

Several city and county recreational departments along the river have established a Yadkin River Trail running from Ferguson to High Rock Lake. This section has been recognized as a state water trail.

Topo Maps: Buffalo Cove, Lenoir, Grandin, Boomer, Purlear, Wilkesboro, Roaring River, Ronda, Elkin South, Elkin North, Copeland, Siloam, Pinnacle, Vienna, Clemmons, Farmington, Advance, Welcome, Churchland, Salisbury

Counties: Caldwell, Wilkes, Yadkin, Forsyth, Davie, Davidson, Rowan

(1) NC 268 bridge at Patterson to NC 268 bridge northeast of Patterson School

Drop: 53′	**Time:** 2 hrs.
Difficulty: 1-2	**Scenery:** B
Distance: 4.2 mi.	**Water Quality:** Fair

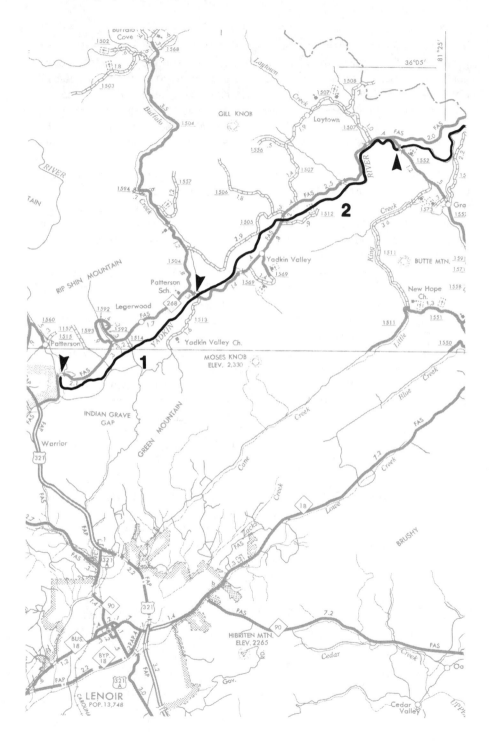

Gauge: USGS gauge is located 50 yards above NC 268 bridge in Patterson, on the east bank. Minimum reading for solo is 1.28.

Difficulties: None, but the river narrows considerably just below the put-in, so the possibility of blocked passages always exists.

(2) NC 268 bridge northeast of Patterson School to Caldwell County Rt. 1509 bridge (Grandin Road)

Drop: 59′	**Time:** 2.5 hrs.
Difficulty: 1-2	**Scenery:** B
Distance: 6.2 mi.	**Water Quality:** Fair

Gauge: Can be run all year. Would be tight through a couple of shoals in very dry periods.

Difficulties: None.

(3) Caldwell County Rt. 1509 bridge (Grandin Road) to the end of Wilkes County Rt. 1137 on Kerr Scott Lake

Drop: 29′	**Time:** 4 hrs.
Difficulty: 1-2	**Scenery:** B
Distance: 9.5 mi.	**Water Quality:** Fair

Gauge: Can be run all year.

Difficulties: None.
There are several Corps of Engineer campgrounds on Kerr Scott.

(4) Wilkes County Rt. 1137 on W. Kerr Scott Reservoir to dam

Drop: 0	**Time:** 3.5 hrs.
Difficulty: A	**Scenery:** A-B
Distance: 6.5 mi.	**Water Quality:** Good

Gauge: None.

Difficulties: Purely physical--carrying around the dam. Pull out on the right of dam abutment and carry about 300 yards to canoe launch site below dam. Do not drag canoes on grass.

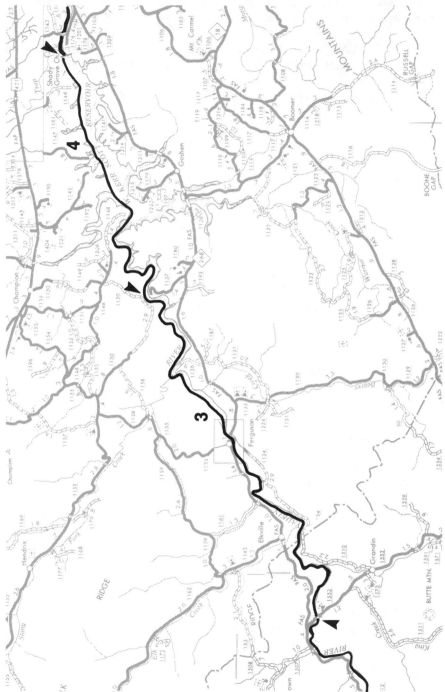

(5) Below W. Kerr Scott Dam, off Wilkes County Rt. 1178 at the tailwater access area, to Smoot Park access area upstream from NC 115 bridge

Drop: 18′
Difficulty: 1-2
Distance: 6.3 mi.

Time: 2.5 hrs.
Scenery: A-B-C
Water Quality: Good

Gauge: None. Runnable year round except during extremely dry conditions.

Difficulties: None.

(6) Smoot Park access area upstream from NC 115 bridge to Wilkes County Rt. 2327 bridge at Roaring River

Drop: 32′
Difficulty: 1-2
Distance: 9.1 mi.

Time: 3.5 hrs.
Scenery: B
Water Quality: Fair

Gauge: See section 5.

Difficulties: Low rock dam on upstream end and to the right of the island located about four and a half miles downstream. Can be run through the break just off the island.

(7) Wilkes County Rt. 2327 bridge at Roaring River to Ronda access area off NC 268 in Ronda

Drop: 16′
Difficulty: 1
Distance: 7.1 mi.

Time: 2.5 hrs.
Scenery: B
Water Quality: Fair

Gauge: See section 5.

Difficulties: None.
Good campsite at normal water levels on gravel bar about four miles downstream.

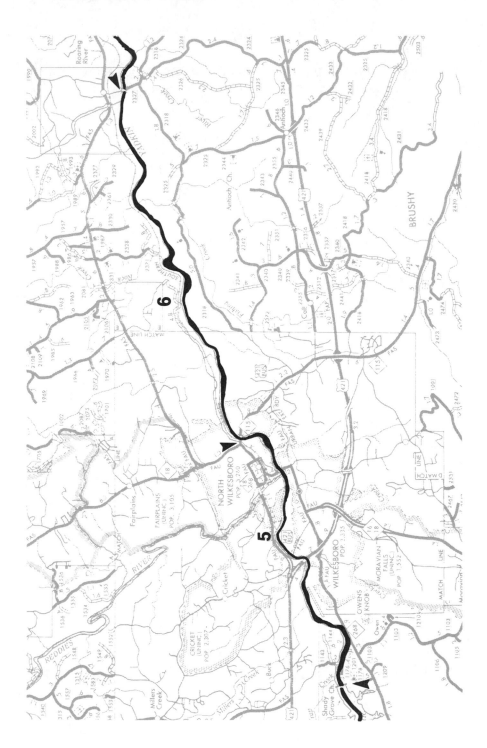

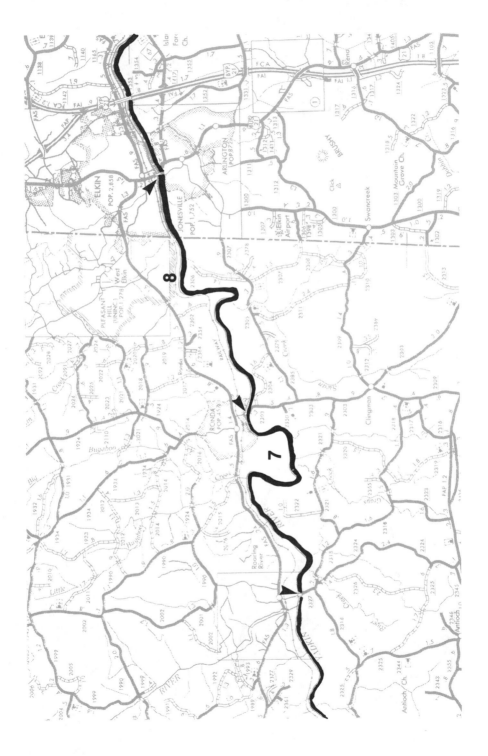

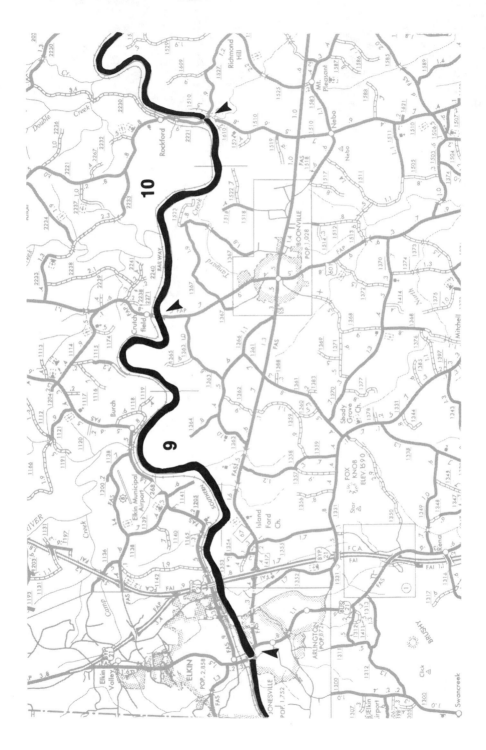

(8) Ronda access area off NC 268 in Ronda to Crater Park access area, downstream from US 21 bridge in Elkin

Drop: 20′
Difficulty: 1
Distance: 7.4 mi.

Time: 2.5 hrs.
Scenery: A-B-C
Water Quality: Fair

Gauge: See section 5.

Difficulties: None.

(9) Crater Park access area, downstream from US 21 bridge in Elkin, to US 601 bridge

Drop: 32′
Difficulty: 1-2
Distance: 10.7 mi.

Time: 4 hrs.
Scenery: A-B-C
Water Quality: Fair

Gauge: See section 5.

Difficulties: None. There are a couple of long shoals on this run.
Good campsites just beyond junction of Mitchell River about four and a half miles downstream.

(10) US 601 bridge to Yadkin County Rt. 1510 bridge at Rockford

Drop: 22′
Difficulty: 1-2
Distance: 5.2 mi.

Time: 2 hrs.
Scenery: A-B
Water Quality: Fair

Gauge: None. Runnable all year. Mandatory portage of some 200 yards around Rt. 1510 low-water bridge if continuing.

Difficulties: None.

(11) Yadkin County Rt. 1510 bridge at Rockford to Rt. 1003 bridge at Siloam

Drop: 28′
Difficulty: 1-2
Distance: 7.9 mi.

Time: 2.5 hrs.
Scenery: A-B
Water Quality: Fair

Gauge: None. Runnable all year.

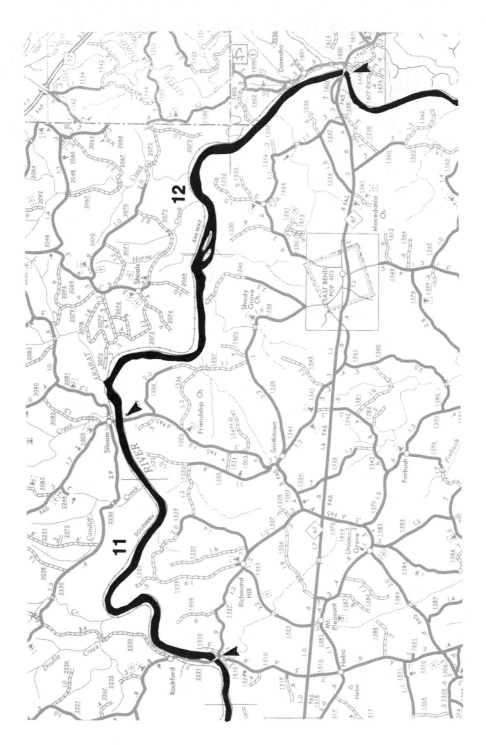

Difficulties: None, except a series of shoals running about a half mile.

(12) Yadkin County Rt. 1003 bridge at Siloam to NC 67 (Donnaha) bridge

Drop: 62′
Difficulty: 1-2
Distance: 11.3 mi.

Time: 4.5 hrs.
Scenery: A-B
Water Quality: Fair

Gauge: None. Runnable all year.

Difficulties: After entering Pilot Mountain State Park (north bank) about four miles downstream, a series of shoals (Bean Shoals) begins and runs for over one and a half miles. A number of islands present many possible passages. This section should be approached with caution at higher water levels.

There are two primitive campsites on the largest island. A camping area for youth groups is located a short distance from the river on the north side. A small fee is charged. Contact the park superintendent for reservations.

(13) NC 67 (Donnaha) bridge to Forsyth County Rt. 1525 bridge

Drop: 23′
Difficulty: 1
Distance: 6.2 mi.

Time: 2 hrs.
Scenery: B
Water Quality: Fair

Gauge: None. Runnable all year.

Difficulties: None.

(14) Forsyth County Rt. 1525 bridge to NC 1001 bridge (Shallowford Road)

Drop: 12′
Difficulty: 1
Distance: 5.3 mi.

Time: 2 hrs.
Scenery: B
Water Quality: Fair

Gauge: None. Runnable all year.

Difficulties: None.

(15) NC 1001 bridge (Shallowford Road) to US 158 bridge

Drop: 21′
Difficulty: 1-2
Distance: 11 mi.
Gauge: None. Runnable all year

Time: 4 hrs.
Scenery: B
Water Quality: Fair

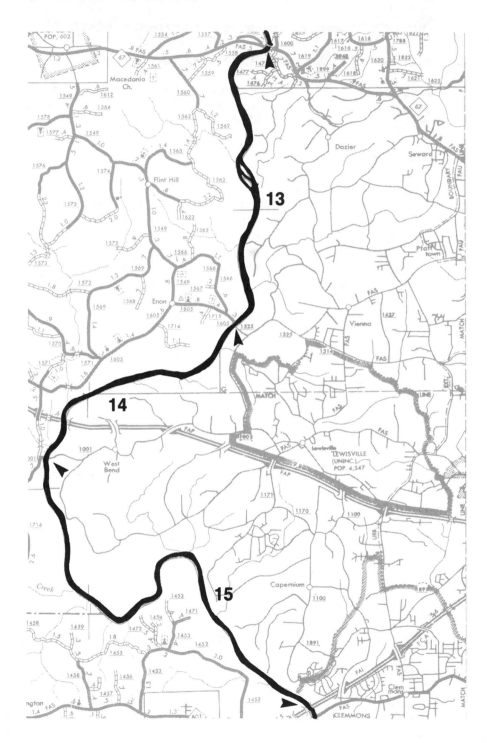

Difficulties: None, except a small rock barricade which has several possible breaks that can be run.

(16) US 158 bridge to US 64 bridge

Drop: 22′
Difficulty: B-1-2
Distance: 17.7 mi.

Time: 6.5 hrs.
Scenery: A-B
Water Quality: Fair

Gauge: None. Runnable all year.

Difficulties: Idols Dam, about four miles downstream, is just below a railroad bridge. Carry on the right. At low-water levels steps left of center can be used for a shorter haul.

A dam, the remains of an historic old mill, is located about ten miles downstream. The shoals here might build up waves that could swamp loaded boats at higher water levels.

(17) US 64 bridge to Concord Church wildlife access area to the end of Davie County Rt. 1832 off NC 801.

Drop: 8′
Difficulty: B-1
Distance: 10.5 mi.

Time: 4 hrs.
Scenery: A-B
Water Quality: Fair

Gauge: None. Runnable all year.

Difficulties: None. Historic Cooleemee Plantation is passed on the west bank.

(18) Concord Church wildlife access area at the end of Davie County Rt. 1832 off NC 801 to NC 150/US 29-70 bridge at the York Hill access area

Drop: 10′
Difficulty: B-1
Distance: 13.2 mi.

Time: 5 hrs.
Scenery: A-B
Water Quality: Fair

Gauge: None. Runnable all year.

Difficulties: None.

Boone's Cave State Park is located about four miles downstream on the east bank. The cave is where Daniel supposedly hid from the Indians at times.

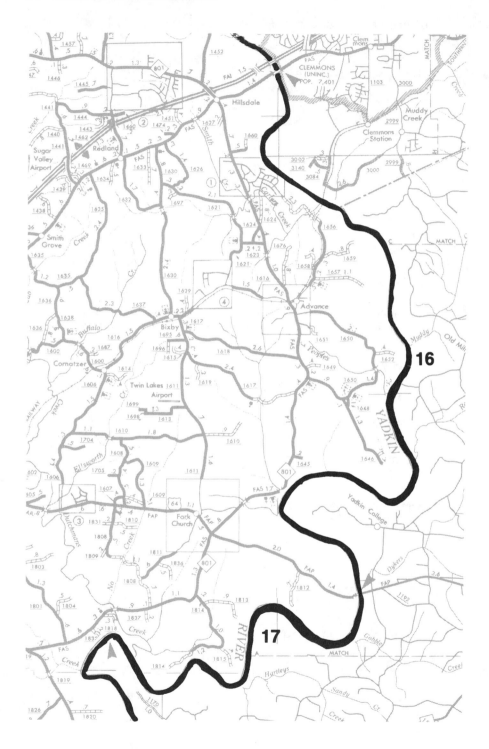

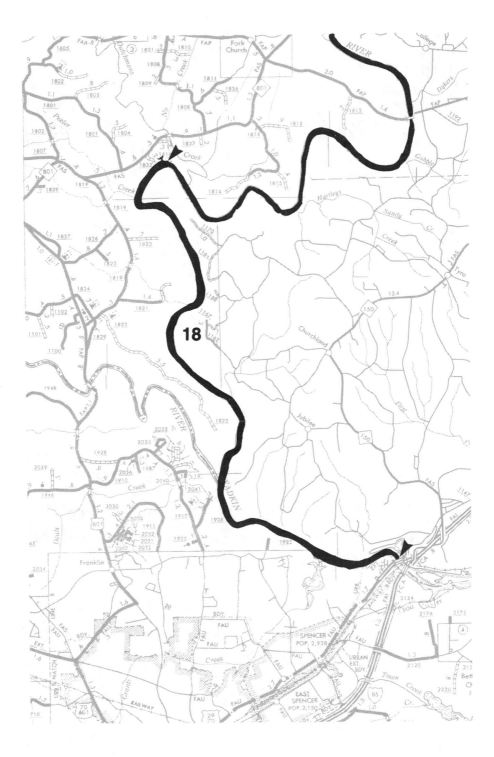

Yadkin River, with Pilot Mountain in the background

There is a reproduction of the cabin built by the Boones here also. An access ramp is planned for development in the future.

For those who might wish to continue their trip, the following information may prove useful. It is 19 miles from US 29-70 bridge down the lake to High Rock Dam; 8.5 miles from the dam to NC 49 bridge; and 11.4 miles from there to Badin Dam. A short distance below Badin Dam, the Uwharrie River enters Lake Tillery. At this point the Yadkin has completed its journey and the Pee Dee is formed. As for Lake Tillery, we are speaking of waterskiing country here.

A map of the river trail is available from the Yadkin River Trail Association, 280 South Liberty Street, Winston-Salem, NC 27101.

2
Cape Fear Basin

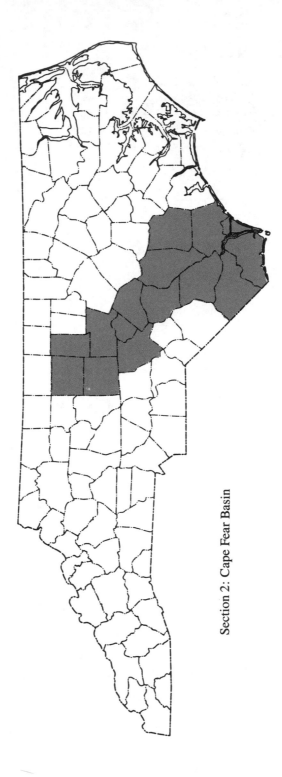

Section 2: Cape Fear Basin

Black River

Little Coharie Creek, Great Coharie Creek, and Six Runs Creek join to form the Black River in Sampson County. The Black flows southeast to the Cape Fear above Wilmington.

The Black is a fairly slow-moving, black water swamp river. Its banks are generally quite low but an occasional bluff will rise up to 15 feet or so above the lower floor. The river gives one a feeling of remoteness although a few isolated cottages and camps appear.

Permission should be obtained from landowners before camping along the banks.

Topo Maps: Garland, Whitelake, Atkinson, Acme

Counties: Sampson, Bladen, Pender

(1) Sampson County Rt. 1134 bridge on Great Coharie Creek to NC 411 bridge at Clear Run

Drop: 9′
Difficulty: A
Distance: 7.2 mi.

Time: 3 hrs.
Scenery: A
Water Quality: Good

Gauge: USGS gauge at NC 411 bridge. Runnable except during dry seasons.

Difficulties: Possible downed trees.

(2) NC 411 bridge at Clear Run to NC 41 bridge

Drop: 8′
Difficulty: A-B
Distance: 6.8 mi.

Time: 3 hrs.
Scenery: A
Water Quality: Good

Gauge: USGS gauge at NC 411 bridge. Runnable year round except following extremely dry spells.

Difficulties: Possible downed trees.

(3) NC 41 bridge to Sampson County Rt. 1007 bridge (Newkirk's Bridge)

Drop: 5'	**Time:** 2.5 hrs.
Difficulty: A-B	**Scenery:** A
Distance: 6.5 mi.	**Water Quality:** Good

Gauge: Runnable year round.

Difficulties: None.

(4) Sampson County Rt. 1007 bridge (Newkirk's Bridge) to wildlife access area off Rt. 1100 about 0.5 mile south of Ivanhoe

Drop: 4'	**Time:** 3.5 hrs.
Difficulty: B	**Scenery:** A
Distance: 8.4 mi.	**Water Quality:** Good

Gauge: Runnable year round.

Difficulties: None.

(5) Wildlife access area off Sampson County Rt. 1100 about 0.5 mile south of Ivanhoe to Bladen County Rt. 1550 bridge

Drop: 5'	**Time:** 3 hrs.
Difficulty: B	**Scenery:** A
Distance: 8.1 mi.	**Water Quality:** Good

Gauge: Runnable year round.

Difficulties: None.
The South River enters from the right about five miles downstream.

(6) Bladen County Rt. 1550 bridge to wildlife access area at Hunt's Bluff, 1 mile south of NC 53 on Rt. 1547

Drop: 7'	**Time:** 4.5 hrs.
Difficulty: B	**Scenery:** A
Distance: 12.2 mi.	**Water Quality:** Good

Gauge: Runnable year round.

Difficulties: None.

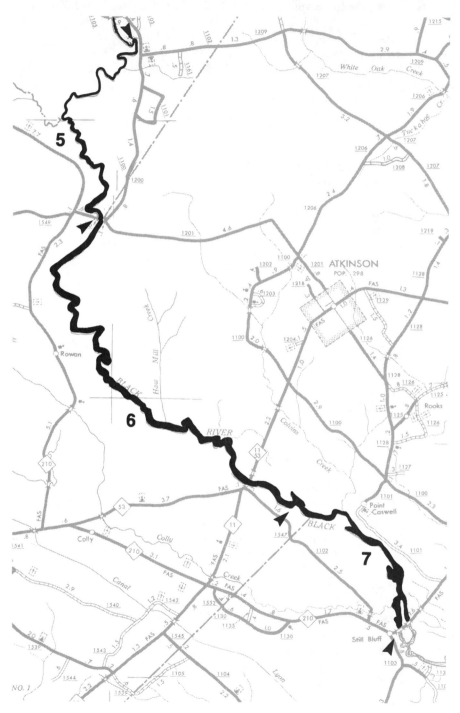

(7) Wildlife access area at Hunt's Bluff, 1 mile south of NC 53 on Bladen County Rt. 1547, to NC 210 bridge (Still Bluff)

Drop: 0′	**Time:** 2.5 hrs.
Difficulty: B-C	**Scenery:** A
Distance: 5 mi.	**Water Quality:** Good

Gauge: Runnable year round.

Difficulties: None, except several large sluices where it may be difficult to determine current and the correct passage.

For those who may wish to extend their trip for the length of the Black, it is approximately 19 miles to the Cape Fear and another 11.8 miles to US 421 bridge in Wilmington. There is little high ground farther down.

Another possible alternative would be to paddle to Moores Creek and up the creek to Moores Creek Military Park and 210 bridge (see Moores Creek).

Cape Fear River

We are told there is a spot about one mile east of Kernersville, just inside Forsyth County, where one with a strong arm can throw a rock into Reedy Fork Creek, one of the heads of the Haw. Then by turning directly around, he can throw another into a nearby spring, the head of the Deep.

The Cape Fear River is formed by the confluence of the Haw and the Deep in the southeast corner of Chatham County. It begins its journey to the sea as a backwater of Buckhorn Dam.

Along its course it meanders through a broad valley, "the Valley of the Highlanders," named for the Scots who settled here. It flows past farm and forest, over the remains of locks and dams built in the early years of the nation, near Revolutionary and Civil War sites, and by a state park. Too much of North Carolina's past occurred along the river to delve into here in any detail.

Below the dam there are occasional rapids for the next 30 miles. The river then becomes flat in Cumberland County and below Fayetteville is controlled by three navigation locks and dams.

Topo Maps: *USGS Topos 7.5"*--Moncure, Cokesbury, Mamers, Lillington, Coats, Erwin, Wade, Solcomb, Vander; *USGS Topos 15"*--St. Pauls, Bladenboro, Elizabethtown, White Lake, Bolton, Acme; *Photo 7.5"*--Castle Hayne, Wilmington

Counties: Chatham, Harnett, Cumberland, Bladen, Pender, Columbus, New Hanover

(1) US 1 bridge over the Haw or Deep rivers to end of Chatham County Rt. 1921 at Buckhorn Dam

Drop: 2′ **Time:** 3 hrs.
Difficulty: A **Scenery:** Poor
Distance: 8 mi. **Water Quality:** Poor

Gauge: None. Can be paddled anytime.

Difficulties: Powerboats.

If you put in on the Haw, you can paddle upstream to the base of Jordan Dam for a look before paddling downstream. An industrial area lies along the Haw and Cape Fear in the vicinity of McKay Island, and when weather conditions trap smoke over the river, it can be unpleasant paddling through here.

On the Deep just below the put-in is the place where soldiers under General Cornwallis built a bridge during the American Revolution. The Cape

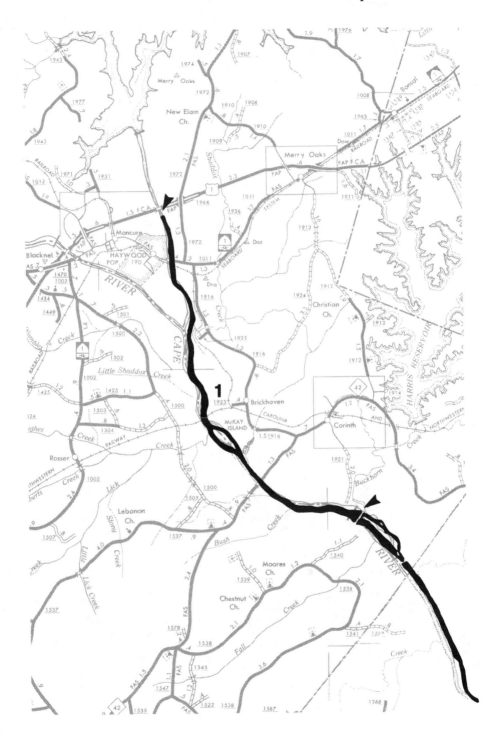

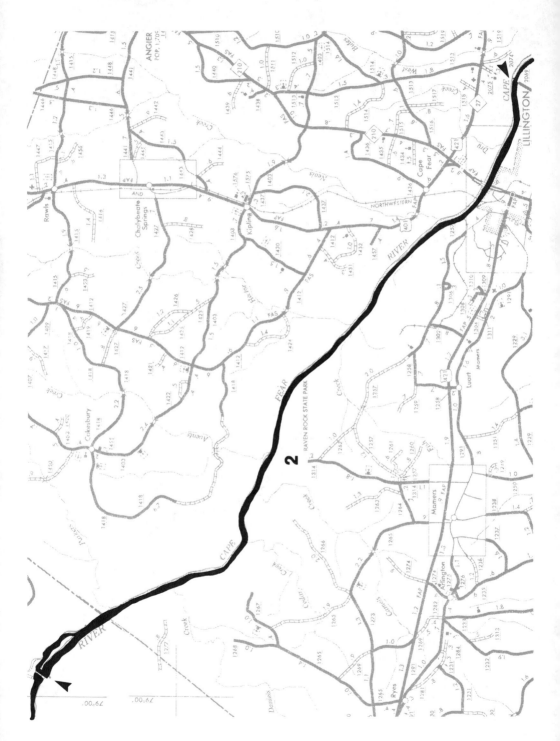

Fear is rich in history, having been used for transportation from earliest colonial days. In the 1850s a series of locks and dams were constructed that made travel possible from the coast as far upriver as Carbonton. Most of the rapids on the Cape Fear are remains of those dams, and at low water the outlines of other water control structures are evident.

Where Chatham County Rt. 2 crosses the Cape Fear there is a boating access area, which makes a convenient access for canoeists.

The dirt road leading down to the old Buckhorn hydro dam is very bad and probably impossible for most cars in wet weather. Do not approach Buckhorn Dam in midstream because water flows across the top; get to the left for an easy lift over. At high water there will be an absolute keeper hydraulic below the dam.

(2) Buckhorn Dam, end of Chatham County Rt. 1921, to wildlife access area at end of Harnett County Rt. 2069

Drop: 30'
Difficulty: 1-2/3
Distance: 16 mi.

Time: 9 hrs.
Scenery: A-B
Water Quality: Fair

Gauge: None. Runnable except after prolonged drought.

Difficulties: Extending entirely across the river below the dam is a rock garden known locally as Buckhorn Falls. At high water it has huge waves and becomes Class 3+. Five miles downstream is a ledge, Lanier Falls, Class 2+, which marks the boundary of Raven Rock State Park.

Another mile farther is a long rapid, "The Fishtraps," Class 2+; run left to right between two islands.

Soon you come to the rock cliffs on the right that give the park its name. Continue past them another half mile to reach a canoe camping area which is *not* accessible by road.

There are a couple of access points near Lillington, but the easiest is two miles past the US 401 bridge at a boating access ramp, reached by taking Rt. 2016.

(3) Wildlife access area at end of Harnett County Rt. 2069 to NC 217 bridge near Erwin

Drop: 40'
Difficulty: 1-2/3
Distance: 8 mi.

Time: 2.5 hrs.
Scenery: A
Water Quality: Fair

Gauge: On NC 217 bridge; 0 to 1.5' can be run except after prolonged drought; powerful Class 2/3 at high water above 2'.

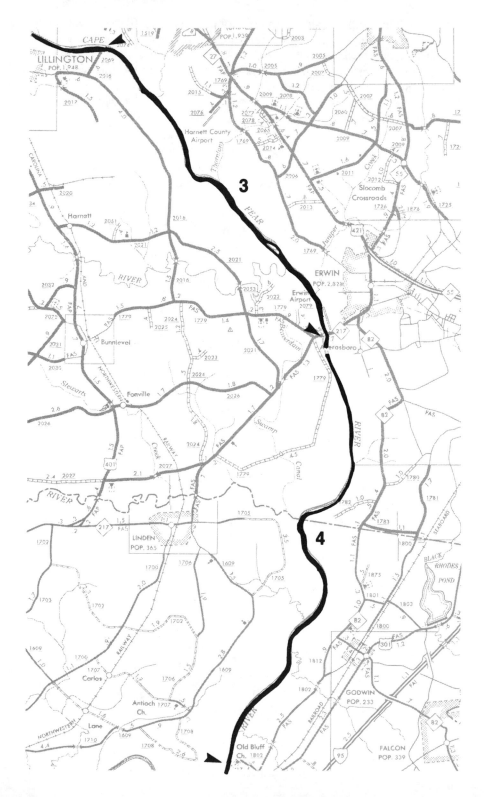

Difficulties: The best whitewater on the Cape Fear begins about four miles into this section where a line of boulders stretches entirely across the left. All the damsites have been indicated by the small blue and white tags of the American Canal Society.

In the next two miles is a series of low ledges that require two dams, Green Rock and Haw Ridge, to make them navigable.

The most difficult rapid is marked by a house-sized boulder just below the confluence with the Upper Little River. At higher water levels the center of the river will be Class 3, but for those seeking an easy route, stay to the right side near a rock island where "Connie's Chute" will carry you past the most difficult rapids.

(4) NC 217 bridge near Erwin to Old Bluff Church, end of Cumberland County Rt. 1709

Drop: 15′   **Time:** 4 hrs.
Difficulty: 1-2   **Scenery:** B
Distance: 10 mi.   **Water Quality:** Fair

Gauge: Route 217 bridge; 0 is minimum; runnable year round.

Difficulties: None. The most difficult rapid is the one underneath the NC 217 bridge; it is best done on the far right. Several smaller rapids in the next three miles, then flat thereafter.

Be sure you can locate your take-out from the river! Old Bluff Church, founded in the mid 1700s, is an historic site of the area. Though used only for special occasions, the grounds and building are well maintained. A hundred yards left from the church starts a set of steps leading down to the river. This is a difficult carry, but the only one for many miles. Remember this is private property and show respect.

Also, you may want to inspect the historic markers placed along NC 82, the shuttle route, which document the course of the Civil War Battle of Avreysboro.

(5) Old Bluff Church, end of Cumberland County Rt. 1709, to Pope Park in Fayetteville at US 301 bridge.

Drop: 15′   **Time:** 8 hrs.
Difficulty: A-B   **Scenery:** B
Distance: 15.4 mi.   **Water Quality:** Fair

Gauge: Route 217 bridge; runnable year round.

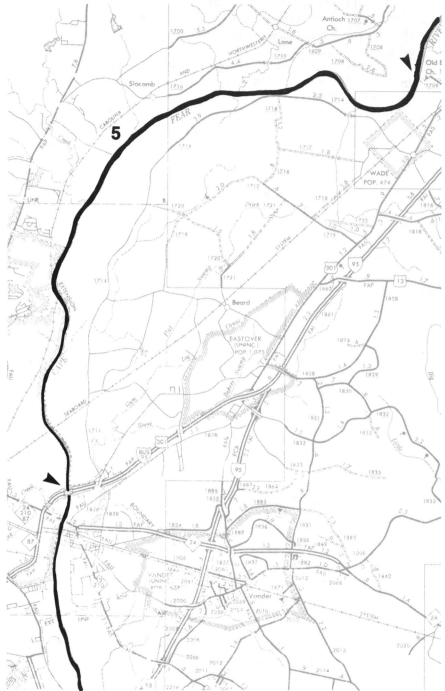

Difficulties: None. The last of the "shallows" occurs about nine miles into the trip. After that, small fishing boats are likely to be encountered.

(6) Pope Park in Fayetteville at US 301 bridge to Huske Lock off Bladen County Rt. 1355

Drop: 8 ′
Difficulty: A
Distance: 20 mi.

Time: 10 hrs.
Scenery: B
Water Quality: Fair

Gauge: None. Runnable year round.

Difficulties: None. There is a boating access ramp about two miles below Pope Park accessible from NC 87. After that there are really no practical accesses until Huske Lock, which is accessible from NC 87, just one mile into Bladen County. Get to the river right when approaching and stay away from the center of the dam; carry around through the part on the right.

Cape Fear River

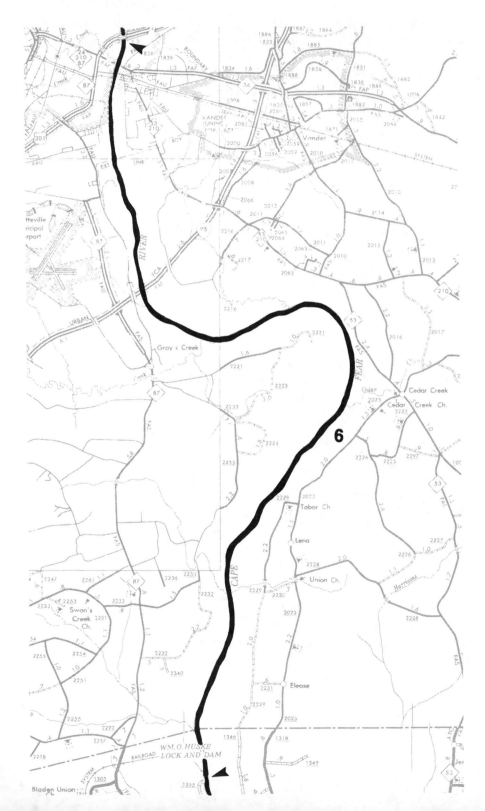

(7) Huske Lock off Bladen County Rt. 1355 to Rt. 1316 bridge near Tar Heel

Drop: 0'   **Time:** 3 hrs.
Difficulty: A   **Scenery:** B
Distance: 7 mi.   **Water Quality:** Fair

Gauge: Runnable year round.

Difficulties: None.

(8) Bladen County Rt. 1316 bridge near Tar Heel to US 701 bridge at Elizabethtown

Drop: 0'   **Time:** 6 hrs.
Difficulty: A   **Scenery:** B
Distance: 14 mi.   **Water Quality:** Fair

Gauge: Runnable year round.

Difficulties: None.

(9) US 701 bridge at Elizabethtown to Bladen County Rt. 1730, Ewell's Ferry, near Carvers

Drop: 10'   **Time:** 9 hrs.
Difficulty: A   **Scenery:** B
Distance: 20 mi.   **Water Quality:** Fair

Gauge: Runnable year round.

Difficulties: Lock Number 2, Brown's Landing, is two miles below the put-in.

(10) Bladen County Rt. 1730, Ewell's Ferry, near Carvers, to Lock Number 1 at Kings Bluff at end of Rt. 1734

Drop: 10'   **Time:** 3 hrs.
Difficulty: A   **Scenery:** B
Distance: 9 mi.   **Water Quality:** Fair

Gauge: Runnable year round.

Difficulties: None.

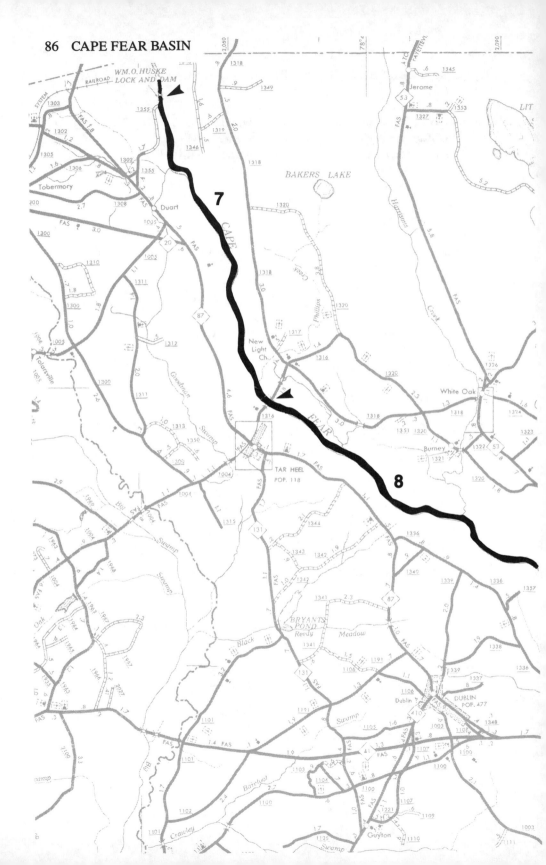

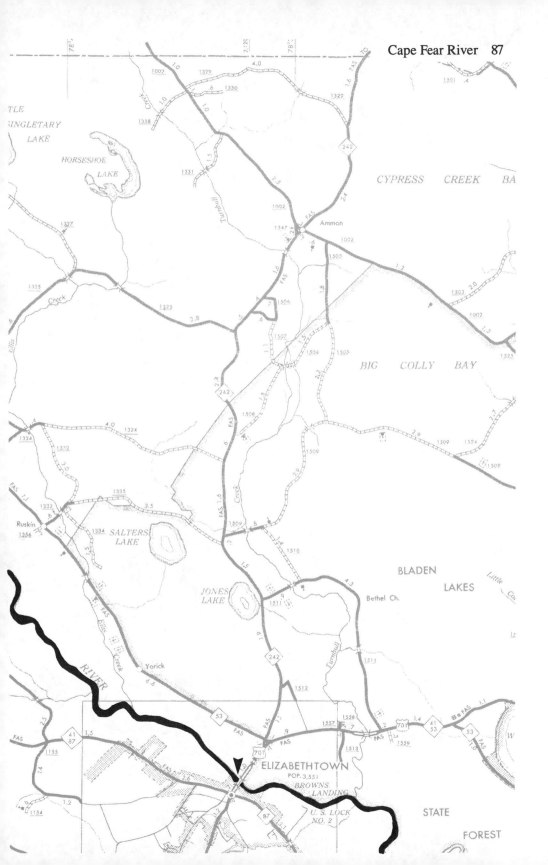

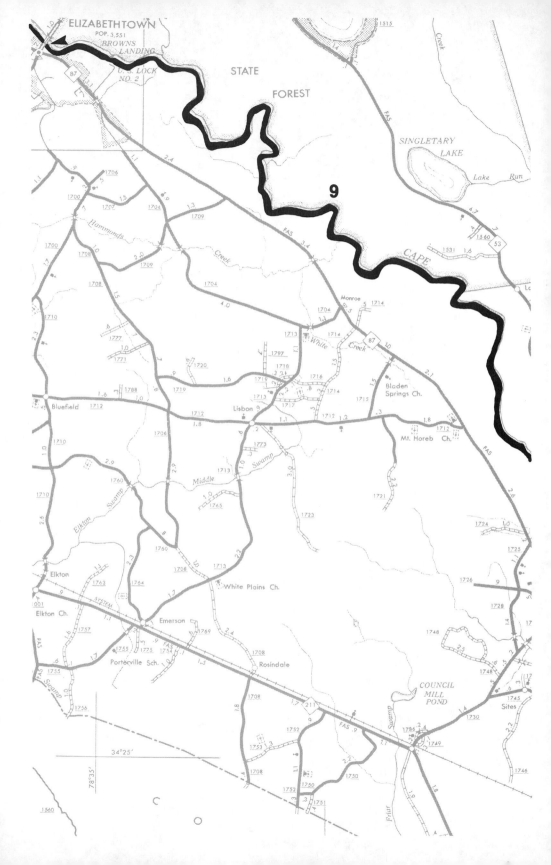

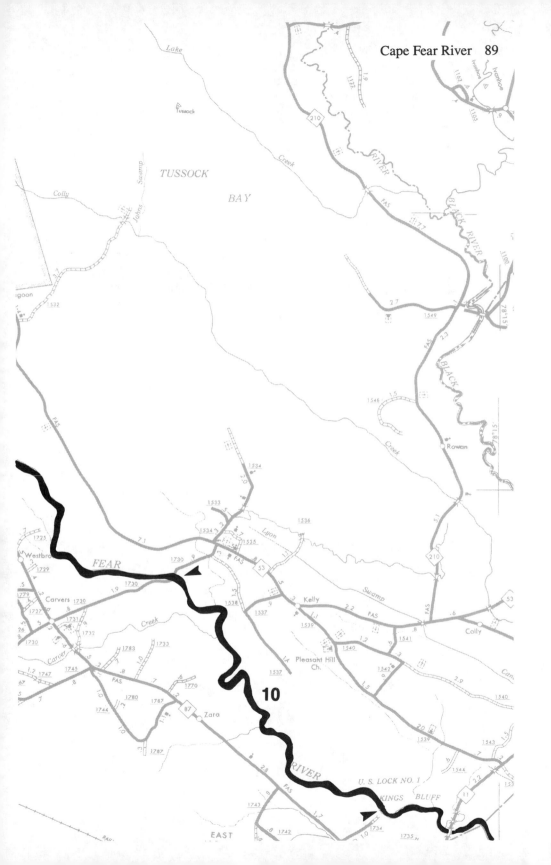

10

(11) Lock Number 1 at Kings Bluff at end of Bladen County Rt. 1734 to US 421 bridge at Wilmington

Drop: 10′   **Time:** 12 hrs.
Difficulty: A   **Scenery:** B
Distance: 28 mi.   **Water Quality:** Fair

Gauge: Runnable year round.

Difficulties: None. NC 141 bridge is about two miles below the put-in. After that, no good access points are reached until just above US 421 bridge. There has been dredging to maintain a channel for shipping, and cutoffs have been made through several bends. Camping sites are problematic depending on water levels. Take-out can be made in the area of 421 bridge or downstream a ways at historic Chandler's Wharf.

Deep River

One of the two major rivers that form the Cape Fear, the Deep heads up between Greensboro and Kernersville and flows in a southeasterly direction. It is always muddy and flows over many shallow, rocky stretches. From earliest days it has been used to turn mill wheels, generate power, and flush waste from the Piedmont. None of the old dams are presently in use. During very high water, the Deep has been explored as high as US 29A-70A in Guilford County. It is small and subject to downed trees.

Topo Maps: *USGS 7.5'* — Randleman, Grays Chapel, Ramseur, Colon, Coleridge, Bennette, Robbins, Putman, White Hill, Goldston, Merry Oaks (most of Jordan Lake), Moncure (confluence of Deep and Haw)

Counties: Randolph, Moore, Lee, Chatham

(1) Randolph County Rt. 2128 at Worthville to Rt. 2221 bridge in Cedar Falls

Drop: 23'
Difficulty: 1-2/4
Distance: 6 mi.

Time: 3 hrs.
Scenery: B-C
Water Quality: Fair

Gauge: None. Runnable in moderately wet weather. See section 4.

Difficulties: An abandoned hydro dam, 20 feet high with water flowing over the top, about one mile past Rt. 2261 bridge at Central Falls. Portage on left. An eight-foot stone dam near Cedar Falls; lift over on the right and scout the rock garden below. This will be Class 4 at good water flows. Rt. 2221 bridge lies at the foot of these rapids.

(2) Randolph County Rt. 2221 in Cedar Falls to Rt. 2615 bridge in Ramseur

Drop: 30'
Difficulty: 1-2/2+
Distance: 5.4 mi.

Time: 2.5 hrs.
Scenery: B-C
Water Quality: Fair-Poor

Gauge: None. Runnable during moderately wet weather. See section 4.

Difficulties: A dam in Franklinville just upstream from Rt. 2235 bridge can be carried on the right. About 75 yards below on the right is a chute dropping about three feet, a Class 2+. It can be scouted from the road running along the right bank while portaging.

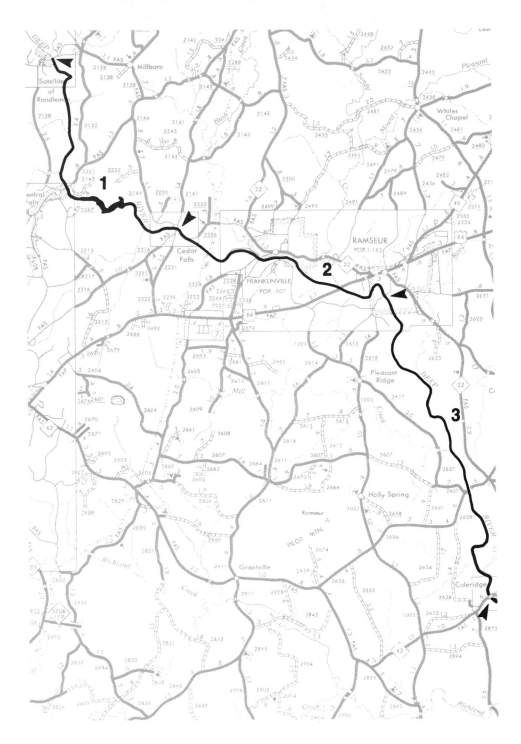

A washed-out dam behind Randolph Mills in Franklinville can be run on the left end. Pull up and scout from the center--or carry if desirable.

A dam about 100 yards below the city park in Ramseur will be seen before being heard. Approach with caution on the right for a fairly easy carry. The dam is some 100 yards above Rt. 2615 bridge. Take-out can be made at the park for those who don't wish to carry around the dam.

(3) Randolph County Rt. 2615 bridge in Ramseur to NC 42 bridge in Coleridge

Drop: 25′	**Time:** 2.75 hrs.
Difficulty: 1	**Scenery:** A-B
Distance: 7.6 mi.	**Water Quality:** Fair

Gauge: USGS gauge 200 yards below the put-in on the right, but it's not very accessible. See section 4.

Difficulties: None. Take-out is on the left side of the dam in Coleridge just below NC 42 bridge. Approach dam with care.

Turtles on Big Swamp

(4) NC 42 bridge in Coleridge to Moore County Rt. 1456 bridge at Howard's Mill

Drop: 35′   **Time:** 4.5 hrs.
Difficulty: 1-2+   **Scenery:** A-B
Distance: 12.7 mi.   **Water Quality:** Good/Fair

Gauge: On Rt. 1456 bridge; +8″ minimum for solo paddling without scraping. Not runnable after a long dry spell.

Difficulties: Put-in above the dam, paddle across the river right, and carry around.
    No major rapids, but many small ledges and rock gardens. Remains of Howard's Mill Dam just above take-out block part of the river, but easily run around the left side, Class 2.

(5) Moore County Rt. 1456 bridge at Howard's Mill to NC 22 bridge at High Falls

Drop: 15′   **Time:** 2.5 hrs.
Difficulty: 1-2/4   **Scenery:** B
Distance: 6.5 mi.   **Water Quality:** Fair

Gauge: See section 4.

Difficulties: Johnson's Ford rapid, about two miles into the trip, is Class 3- and consists of a five-foot drop in two steps. Scout from the right. At about six miles is High Falls Dam. Go toward the left and step out on the island to scout or to portage. The mill sluice on the far left has been run when free of debris, but is dangerous. Scout carefully!

(6) NC 22 bridge at High Falls to Moore County Rt. 1006 bridge at Glendon

Drop: 20′   **Time:** 3.5 hrs.
Difficulty: 1-2   **Scenery:** B
Distance: 9.5 mi.   **Water Quality:** Fair

Gauge: See section 4. This section is fairly flat and requires less water than those above.

Difficulties: None.

(7) Moore County Rt. 1006 bridge at Glendon to NC 42 bridge at Carbonton, Chatham County

Drop: 20′
Difficulty: 1-A
Distance: 11 mi.

Time: 4 hrs.
Scenery: B
Water Quality: Fair

Gauge: None. Runnable year round.

Difficulties: None. Mostly flatwater backed up by the 15-foot dam at Carbonton, which is just below the NC 42 bridge. A boating access area is located two-tenths of a mile above the bridge on the left and is a convenient take-out.

About four miles into the trip, just about Rt. 1621, is a state historic site, the House in the Horseshoe, an old plantation house. In bygone times the produce from this plantation and many others like it was transported by river barge to the markets on the coast.

Cypress knees along the Lumber River

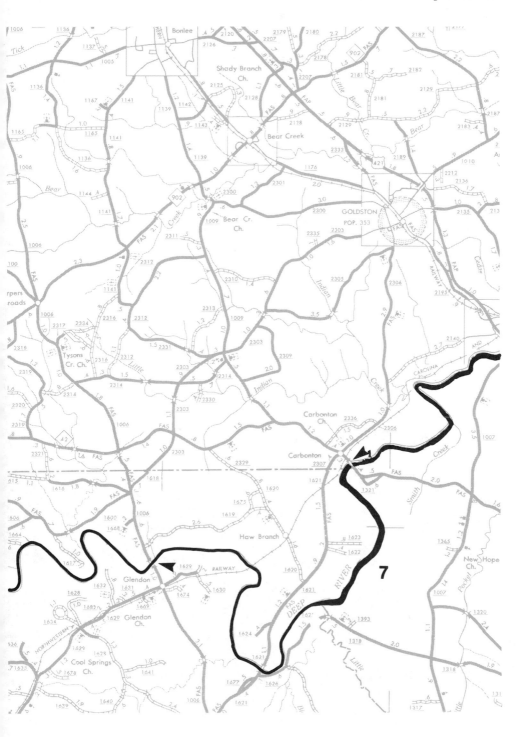

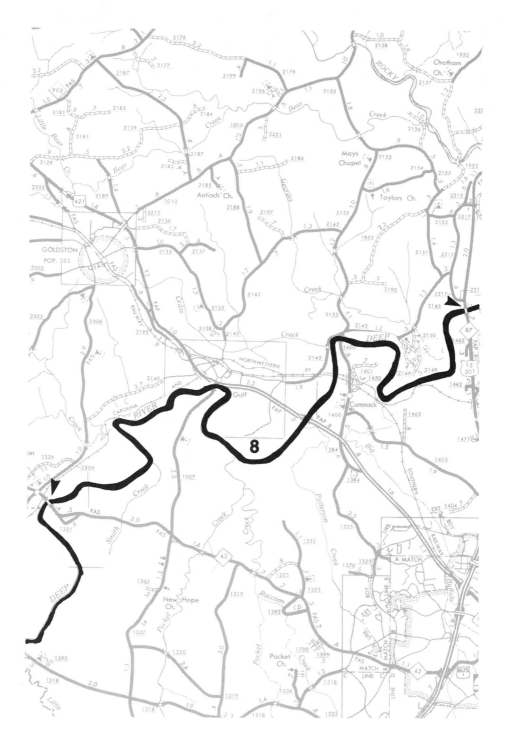

(8) NC 42 bridge at Carbonton, Chatham County, to US 15-501 bridge

Drop: 25′
Difficulty: 1
Distance: 15 mi.

Time: 6 hrs.
Scenery: B-C
Water Quality: Fair

Gauge: None. Runnable year round.

Difficulties: None. Mostly flat.

There are two notable points. Below US 421 bridge are the remains of a dam and sluice built for river navigation. A bit below here, back in the woods to the right, is the Endor Iron Furnace where local ores were smelted during the Civil War.

(9) US 15-501 bridge to US 1 bridge

Drop: 15′
Difficulty: 1-2
Distance: 7 mi.

Time: 2.5 hrs.
Scenery: B
Water Quality: Fair

Gauge: None. Runnable except after a prolonged dry spell.

Difficulties: About one and a half miles into the trip is the confluence with the Rocky River; below here are three easy rock garden rapids. Just above the take-out is a large dam which is perhaps the most difficult portage in the East. The left is generally badly obstructed by debris; the right is preferred. Lift up the cliff, carry a short distance along the edge, then drop boat down 60 feet to relaunch below the dam. *Do not* enter the millrace on the left as water flows through the wheelhouse, creating a death trap. Take-out is easiest on the right just below the bridge.

(10) US 1 bridge to NC 42 bridge near Corinth

Drop: 10′
Difficulty: A
Distance: 6.5 mi.

Time: 2.5 hrs.
Scenery: B
Water Quality: Poor

Gauge: None. Can be paddled year round. This is flatwater backed up by Buckhorn Dam.

Difficulties: None. Powerboats frequent this area in warm-weather months.

There is a wildlife access area just above NC 42 bridge on river left.

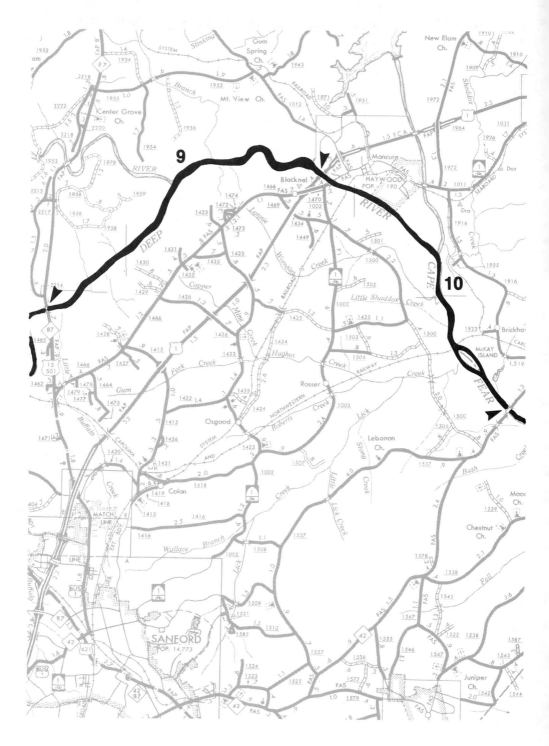

Haw River

The Haw River heads up in northwestern Guilford County, not far from Greensboro, and flows easterly through the industrialized "Piedmont Crescent." Since the early 1800s it has been dammed to provide water power to the many textile factories, which in turn add color and odor. Textile plant wastes are often dumped on Saturday nights because the state pollution control people won't be checking on weekends. The ink-black water extends for miles, staining the rocks before being somewhat diluted. Yet for all its problems, the Haw is still the most popular canoeing river in the Piedmont because of the whitewater. As it falls off the Piedmont Plateau, there are miles of Class 2 and occasionally more difficult rapids. At high water many boats have been lost, and several drownings have occurred.

Topo Maps: Ossipee, Lake Burlington, Burlington, Mebane, Saxapahaw, White Cross, Silk Hope, Bynum, Farrington, New Hope Dam

Counties: Alamance, Chatham

(1) NC 62 bridge at Glencoe to US 54 bridge, Alamance County

Drop: 50′ **Time:** 3 hrs.
Difficulty: 1-2 **Scenery:** C
Distance: 7.6 mi. **Water Quality:** Poor

Gauge: USGS gauging station on left bank at US 70 bridge; 2.5′ minimum for solo.

Difficulties: Decrepit woodland stone dam behind the Cone Mills Factory at Haw River. A four-foot drop can be run, but there are wood and iron sticking up to snag you. Scout!

(2) US 54 bridge, Alamance County, to Saxapahaw Dam, just above Rt. 2171 bridge

Drop: 20′ **Time:** 3 hrs.
Difficulty: 1-2 **Scenery:** C
Distance: 7.6 mi. **Water Quality:** Poor

Gauge: See section 2.

Difficulties: Two stone dams. The first, a rotting wood and stone structure 200 yards below Rt. 2158 bridge at Swepsonville. A four-foot drop

101

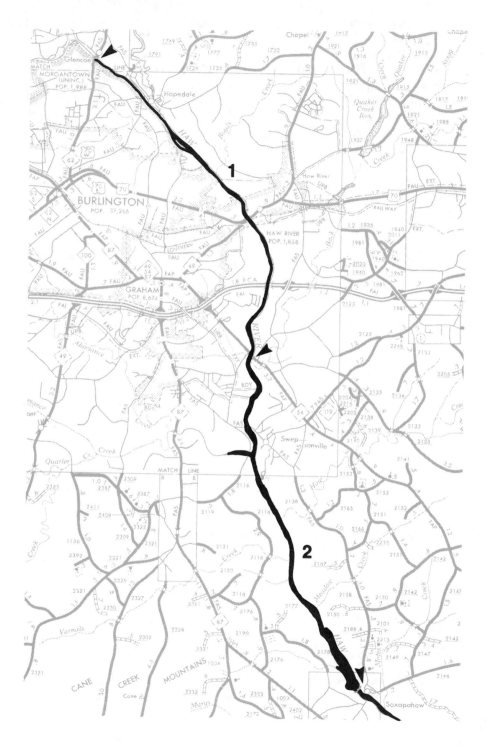

can be run, but wood and iron are sticking up and can spear a boat. Scout from left side.

The second dam is a seven-foot stone hydro dam one mile below Swepsonville. This can be portaged on the left side across an island where the wheelhouse was located.

The lake behind Saxapahaw hydro dam is four miles long. This is a big dam--do not approach the center; get to river left and carry around.

(3) Saxapahaw Dam to Chatham County Rt. 1545 bridge ("Chicken Bridge")

Drop: 30′   **Time:** 2.5 hrs.
Difficulty: 1-2   **Scenery:** C
Distance: 5.5 mi.   **Water Quality:** Poor

Gauge: See section 2.

Difficulties: None.

(4) Chatham County Rt. 1545 bridge ("Chicken Bridge") to Bynum Dam, just upstream of US 15-501 bridge

Drop: 50′   **Time:** 3 hrs.
Difficulty: 1-2   **Scenery:** A-B
Distance: 6.5 mi.   **Water Quality:** Fair

Gauge: There is no convenient gauge for this section of the river. A good guide, however, is to see how many of the bridge's footings are visible. If three can be seen, the river is low and the trip will be long. When none may be seen, the river should not be run by novices. When the river rises to within two to three feet of the concrete cross braces, it should not be run by anyone. This section can be run year round except following an unusually long dry season.

Difficulties: There are only two places of any consequence. The first is about one and seven-tenths miles downstream, where the river makes an abrupt left turn and goes around an island. The rapid on the right is normally entered as close to the island as the overhanging branches will allow. The second rapid is about four miles downstream, after about a mile of pleasant and nearly continuous rapids. The river is quite wide, with an island placed to the left. At low water it is run to the left, and once past the island, the rapids should be traversed to the right to avoid a large boulder about 100 yards downstream. Only one more rapid remains, downstream of the gas line, where the lake starts. Stay on the left side of the river to the take-out just upstream of the dam.

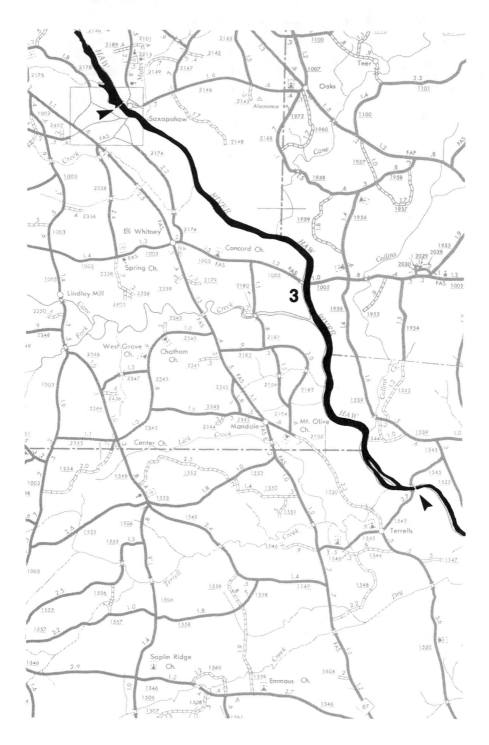

(5) US 15-501 bridge, on the south side of the river and upstream of the bridge, to Route 1943 bridge

Drop: 117′   **Time:** 2.5 hrs.
Difficulty: 1-2-3   **Scenery:** A-B
Distance: 6 mi.   **Water Quality:** Fair

Gauge: The gauge is located on an upstream piling on the north side of US 64 bridge. Minimum for solo is 6″ below 0. Maximum is 1.5′ above 0.

Difficulties: There are many parallel paths that can be taken, but generally the widest part of the river is best for the newcomer. Once past the bridge at Bynum (visible from US 15-501 bridge), one should traverse the river far to the left. A mile from the put-in, the river will be narrow and present three choices of direction. The left channel has a Class 2+ drop consisting of a ledge and rapids immediately below. It is best run through a chute just to the left of the small island, although at high water it can be approached in the center, with a quick S turn required after the first drop.

After some miles, the river becomes flat and very wide. When the water level is higher than zero, the canoeist can paddle to the right, passing through many rocks and tiny islands and taking a series of delightful drops at the extreme right of the river. At the end of these drops is a Class 2+, an S turn, requiring a hard left turn. (At the aforementioned spot one can also remain to the left, going through a long run over a rock field, and approach the center of the US 64 bridge.) Below US 64 bridge, one can remain at the right or go through a narrow slot between two islands about 50 yards downstream of the bridge to get out into the main channel. (The paddler continuing from the left channel may take the right-hand route by moving close to the right just before the bridge and turning back upstream through the narrow slot.)

The advantage of the right channel is that the Lunch Stop Rapid, Class 3, can be run. It is most difficult at low water and is run close to the right, moving to the left just at the bottom to avoid a rock.

Fifty yards below the Lunch Stop Rapid, a left is taken to move out into the main current. The water is heavy with large standing waves. After a run of 200-300 yards, there is a sharp turn to the left followed immediately by a hard right to get into calm water just upstream of Gabriel's Bend.

Gabriel's Bend, a Class 3+, is identified by a large rock wall on the right and may be scouted on the right. Open boats may run it anywhere with the gauge of zero or less. At higher levels the standing waves become large and holes develop, which can easily swamp a canoe. The conservative route is close to the left all the way and very close to the large rock halfway down.

Immediately below Gabriel's Bend, the paddler traverses all the way to the left of the river through some islands where the Haw's Revenge, a Class 3, awaits. It cannot be seen from above and, because of the banks and fast current,

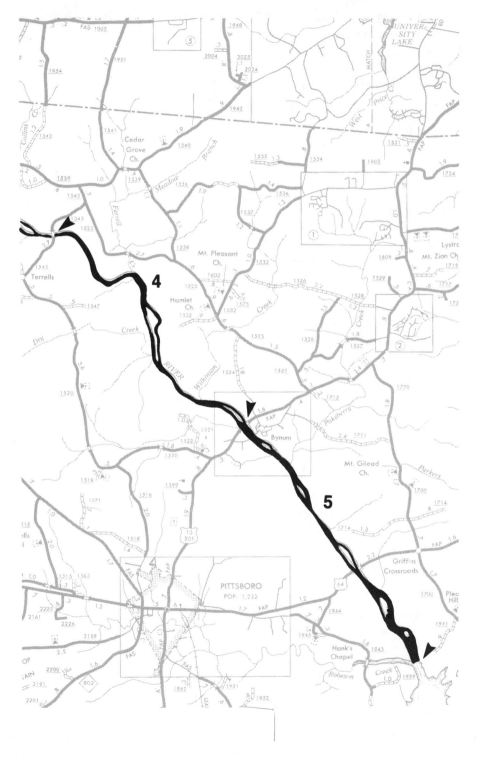

is very hard to scout. It should be entered to the left under overhanging branches; work to keep from being swept to the right. Remain to the left past a large jagged rock, and at the bottom go through some small rocks. The temptation is to take a right before the innocent-looking rocks, but firmly resist. Many boats have been badly mangled there.

The next major drop is approached from the left side of the river and has a number of possible entries. At a gauge reading of one foot, a straight chute appears at the left of a small island. Below that level, one enters at the left but moves quickly to the right of the island, traversing all the way across and exiting at the far right.

After a small but pesky ledge and a wide-open area with a continuous but gradual drop, the Pipeline, a Class 3, is found by remaining generally to the right of the open river, where a straight and fairly narrow section separates off on the right. At the end, there is a turn to the right and one enters the Pipeline. Standing waves are large and holes develop at high gauge readings. Near the end, the rapid does a quick S to the right, going around a large boulder located on the left. Unfortunately for the paddler, where the river is running high the cofferdam downstream of the take-out will create a lake, which often backs up to cover the Pipeline.

The steel bridge can be seen once one is out of the Pipeline, with the take-out on the left directly at the bridge.

Somewhere around this point you will encounter the slack water backed up behind Jordan Dam. Gone are the rapids that once made this such a superb run. You paddle over them to the take-out along the lakeshore.

(6) Jordan Lake

There is no easy way to portage around the dam. You can paddle around the lake to any of several access points. If you want to continue down the Haw and on to the Cape Fear, see Cape Fear River, section 1.

Little River

Draining parts of Moore, Hoke, and Cumberland counties easterly into the Cape Fear, the Little River is a fast-moving Class C flatwater stream flowing through a deep, soil-banked gully. An unusual variety of plants found along the route includes bald cypress, laurel, bamboo, and azalea. Above NC 210, the stream is quite small and swampy in places. The Fort Bragg Military Reservation lies along the right bank. About 15 miles of the river, as far up as Moore County Rt. 2021 bridge near Vass, has been run during wet weather.

Topo Maps: Manchester, Slocomb, Bunn Level, Erwin

Counties: Cumberland, Harnett

(1) NC 210 bridge to US 401 bridge

Drop: 35′	**Time:** 5 hrs.
Difficulty: C	**Scenery:** A
Distance: 14 mi.	**Water Quality:** Good

Gauge: US 401 bridge. Runnable year round. Little change in difficulty from below 0 to over 3′.

Difficulties: Low branches, downed trees, snags. Easy enough for winter paddling. Particularly beautiful in mid-April when the banks are white with the blooms of mountain laurel. The take-out at 401 bridge is steep and sometimes slippery.

(2) US 401 bridge to Old Bluff Church on the Cape Fear River

Drop: 35′	**Time:** 4.5 hrs.
Difficulty: C	**Scenery:** A
Distance: 12 mi.	**Water Quality:** Good

Gauge: See section 1. Runnable year round.

Difficulties: Snags, downed trees. Pretty scenery, big cypress trees. After reaching the Cape Fear it is four miles of flatwater paddling to reach the take-out at Old Bluff Church. See Cape Fear River, section 4 for details.

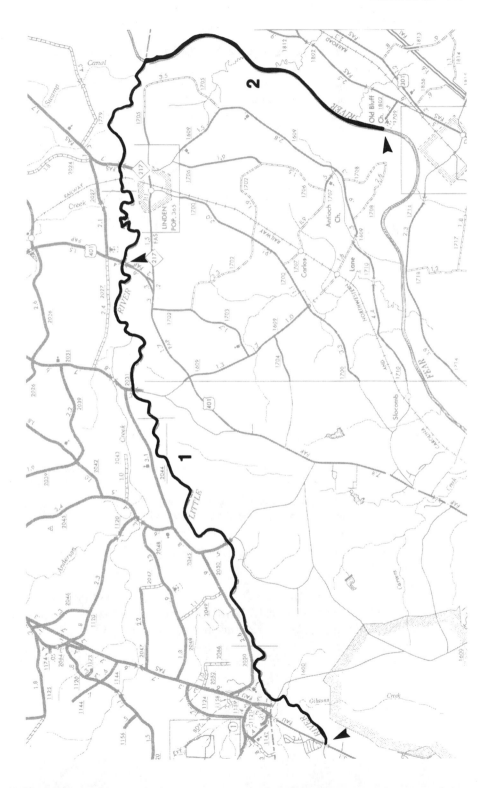

Moores Creek

Moores Creek heads up in west-central Pender County and drains a good portion of that area. Because of the swampy terrain it is generally too narrow to run above the designated put-in point. It continues through the swamp for some distance when the land begins to rise into sandhills on the left.

The first decisive victory of the American Revolution occurred at Widow Moores Creek Bridge on February 27, 1776. North Carolina patriot militia defeated a much larger Loyalist force on its way to meet with a British expeditionary squadron on the coast. This small but crucial battle helped prevent a full-scale invasion of the South and drove North Carolina to instruct its delegation to the Continental Congress to vote for independence--the first state to do so.

The put-in is alongside Moores Creek National Military Park. We highly recommend a visit to the visitor center, followed by a walking tour of the battlefield.

Topo Maps: Acme

County: Pender

(1) NC 210 bridge at Moores Creek National Military Park to The Borough on the Black River

Drop: 0'   **Time:** 2 hrs.
Difficulty: A   **Scenery:** A
Distance: 4.2 mi.   **Water Quality:** Good

Gauge: None. Runnable year round except during very dry seasons.

Difficulties: None. The channel is relatively easy to follow at normal water levels. Locating the take-out in The Borough may be the most difficult part of this trip.

Although these are tidal waters, tides will not be a big factor in estimating paddling time.

Directions: Take-out--East on NC 210 into Currie. Right on first paved road, right on 1115 (continue on 1115 beyond pavement until pavement is reached again). Right on 1137 (you're in the boonies, buddy), then an immediate left, a right up a slight grade, a right again and down about a quarter mile to the Black just downstream from the confluence with Moores Creek. It

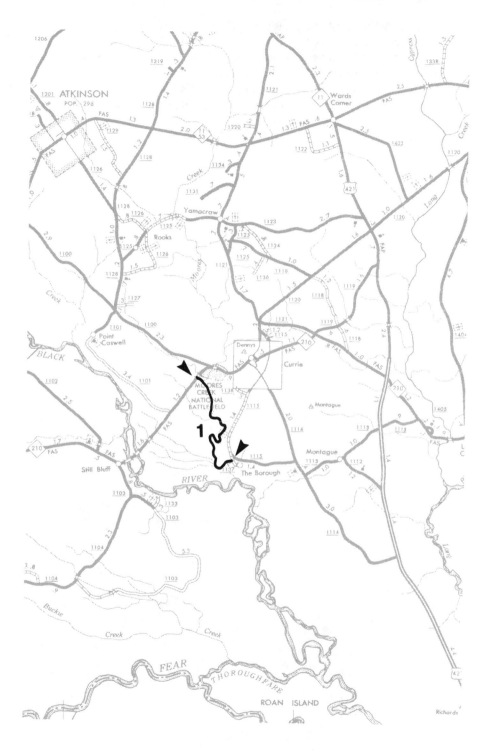

would be best to leave the shuttle car close to the paved road. This is private property but apparently is open for public use at this time.

For those wishing a longer trip, simply turn right upon reaching the Black River and paddle back up two and eight-tenths miles to NC 210 bridge on the Black. If timing is good, one can catch the tide going out on Moores Creek and coming in on the Black. If this decision is made, run the shuttle west on NC 210 for the take-out.

Northeast Cape Fear River

The Northeast Cape Fear River heads up in the extreme southern part of Wayne County and winds its way south across Duplin and Pender counties to confluence with the Cape Fear outside of Wilmington.

It begins as a small, winding stream running over sandy bottoms through a very remote area. As it widens farther along, it courses for some 25 miles along the Angola Bay State Game Preserve where a variety of wildlife may be observed. With the occasional interruption of civilization at access areas, the river keeps its wilderness character for most all its length.

Beyond US 117 it opens up to flow through salt marshes until reaching Wilmington.

Topo Maps: Burgaw, Mooretown, Castle Hayne

Counties: Duplin, Pender, New Hanover

(1) Duplin County Rt. 1700 bridge at Sarecta to wildlife access area at NC 24 bridge

Drop: 5'	**Time:** 2.5 hrs.
Difficulty: B	**Scenery:** A
Distance: 5 mi.	**Water Quality:** Good

Gauge: None. Runnable except for extremely dry spells.

Difficulties: Downed trees which are most likely to be a factor at low water levels.

(2) Wildlife access area at NC 24 bridge to Duplin County Rt. 1961 bridge at Hallsville

Drop: 4'	**Time:** 2.5 hrs.
Difficulty: B	**Scenery:** A
Distance: 5 mi.	**Water Quality:** Good

Gauge: None. Runnable year round.

Difficulties: Possible downed trees.

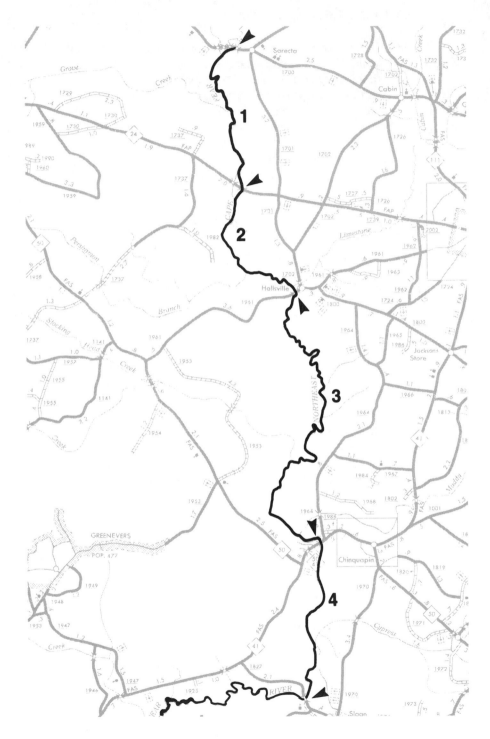

(3) Duplin County Rt. 1961 bridge at Hallsville to NC 50-41 bridge at Chinquapin

Drop: 11 '   **Time:** 3.5 hrs.
Difficulty: B   **Scenery:** A
Distance: 9.1 mi.   **Water Quality:** Good

Gauge: None. Runnable year round.

Difficulties: Possible downed trees.

(4) NC 50-41 bridge at Chinquapin to Duplin County Rt. 1827 (Deep Bottom) bridge

Drop: 5 '   **Time:** 1.75 hrs.
Difficulty: B   **Scenery:** A
Distance: 4.1 mi.   **Water Quality:** Good

Gauge: None. Runnable year round.

Difficulties: Possible downed trees.

Campsite along the Northeast Cape Fear River

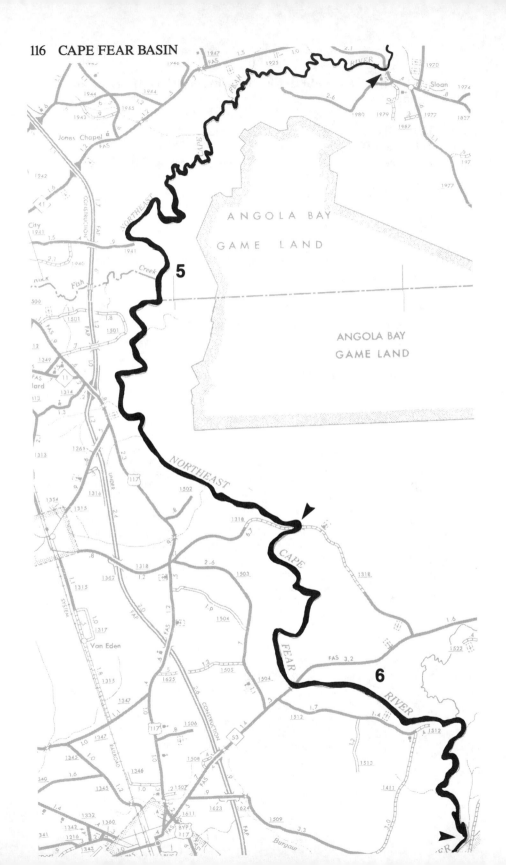

(5) Duplin County Rt. 1827 (Deep Bottom) bridge to Pender County Rt. 1318 (Croom) bridge at Shelter Neck

Drop: 13′
Difficulty: B-C
Distance: 23.7 mi.

Time: 9 hrs.
Scenery: A
Water Quality: Good

Gauge: Painted gauge on Rt. 1318 abutment. If "too wet to plow," we suggest you go home. Runnable year round.

Difficulties: Possible downed trees. Tides can have an effect on paddling times through this section as well as the lower sections.

Campsites should not be difficult to locate unless the water is quite high.

(6) Pender County Rt. 1318 (Croom) bridge at Shelter Neck to Holly Shelter wildlife access area on Rt. 1520

Drop: 5′
Difficulty: B-C
Distance: 11.8 mi.

Time: 4.5 hrs.
Scenery: A-B
Water Quality: Good

Gauge: None.

Difficulties: None.

This section can be cut short (four and a half miles) by taking out at the wildlife access area (Sawpit Landing) at the end of Rt. 1512.

(7) Holly Shelter wildlife access area on Pender County Rt. 1520 to NC 210 bridge

Drop: 3′
Difficulty: C
Distance: 11 mi.

Time: 4-5 hrs.
Scenery: A-B
Water Quality: Good

Gauge: None.

Difficulties: Winds and tides become more of a factor in determining paddling times from here downstream. It would be wise to check times for changing tides.

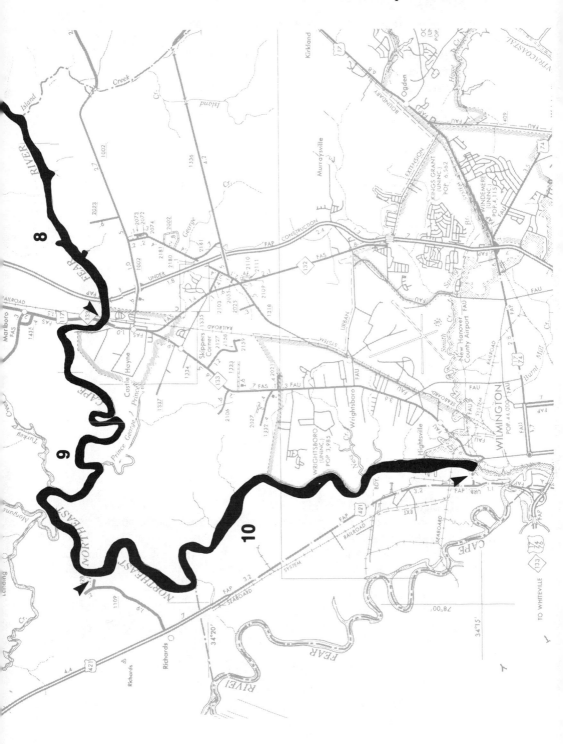

(8) NC 210 bridge to wildlife access area at US 117 bridge

Drop: 0′   **Time:** 4 hrs.
Difficulty: B-A   **Scenery:** A
Distance: 9.3 mi.   **Water Quality:** Good

Gauge: None.

Difficulties: See section 7.

(9) Wildlife access area at US 117 bridge to Cowpen Landing off Pender County Rt. 1109

Drop: 0′   **Time:** 4 hrs.+
Difficulty: B-A   **Scenery:** A
Distance: 10.4 mi.   **Water Quality:** Good

Gauge: None.

Difficulties: See section 7.

(10) Cowpen Landing off Pender County Rt. 1109 to NC 133 bridge in Wilmington

Drop: 0′   **Time:** 4.5 hrs.+
Difficulty: B-A   **Scenery:** A-B-C
Distance: 11.4 mi.   **Water Quality:** Fair

Gauge: None.

Difficulties: See section 7.

Take-out can be made also at historic Chandler's Wharf, a short distance below the bridge on the left.

Sections 8, 9, and 10 run through lowlands, so campsites come few and far between.

Reedy Fork

Reedy Fork* flows eastward across Guilford and Alamance counties to a confluence with the Haw River near Ossipee. North of Greensboro, two major impoundments, Lake Brandt and Townsend Lake, form the greater part of the city water supply. Although the stream can be paddled from US 29 (below the lakes) downstream all the way to the dam at Ossipee, the first and last segments are almost entirely flatwater. The stream flows through rolling wooded countryside with occasional pastureland. Civilization seldom intrudes except at the road crossings and the two mill dams.

Topo Maps: Browns Summit, Ossipee

County: Guilford

(1) Guilford County Rt. 2732 (Hines Chapel Road) bridge to dam just above Rt. 2719 bridge

Drop: 30′ **Time:** 2.5 hrs.
Difficulty: 1-2 **Scenery:** A
Distance: 5.9 mi. **Water Quality:** Good

Gauge: At Rt. 2732 bridge. Minimum for solo is 665 (by extension). Can be run most of the year except during dry spells.

Difficulties: Possible fallen trees; dam at take-out. Take out or portage on left. A road closely parallels the left bank at this point. Some flatwater, with occasional ledges up to Class 2.

(2) Dam just above Guilford County Rt. 2719 bridge to old mill just above NC 61 bridge

Drop: 30′ **Time:** 1.5 hrs.
Difficulty: 1-2 **Scenery:** A
Distance: 4.2 mi. **Water Quality:** Good-Poor

Difficulties: Broken dam shortly before take-out. Can usually be run but should be scouted, as rocks and logs require some maneuvering. Mostly

---

*From the notes of Allen Trelease.

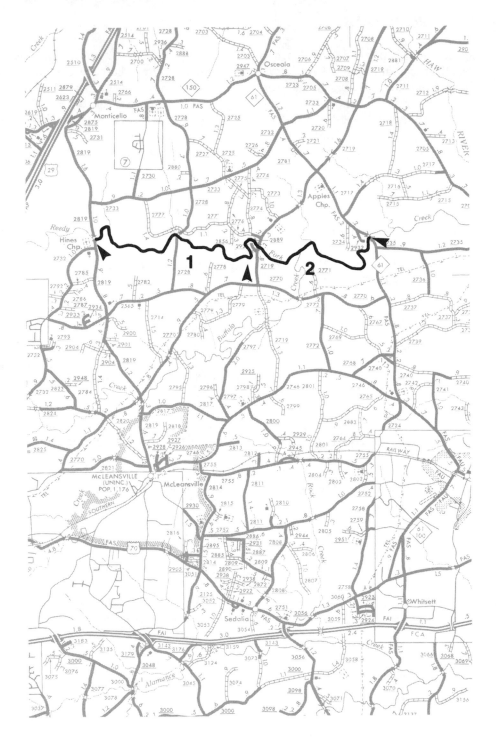

flatwater except for the dam and rapids below. Buffalo Creek, carrying Greensboro's sewage, enters from the right two and seven-tenths miles above the take-out, contributing an additional inducement to scout the dam. The water quality of Buffalo Creek is expected to improve with the completion of new sewage treatment facilities.

Rockfish Creek

Flowing easterly through southern Cumberland County, the Rockfish and Little Rockfish creeks were once impounded to provide waterpower to the factories at Hope Mills, now abandoned. The stream is small and the access difficult, but the scenery makes up for the trouble.

Topo Maps: Saint Pauls

Counties: Cumberland, Bladen

(1) Cumberland County Rt. 1127 bridge to NC 87 bridge

Drop: 28′	**Time:** 3 hrs.
Difficulty: B	**Scenery:** A
Distance: 7 mi.	**Water Quality:** Fair

Gauge: Abandoned USGS gauge at confluence of Rockfish with Little Rockfish, one mile below put-in. Minimum is 3.5. Would only be unrunnable after prolonged drought.

Difficulties: Downed trees, snags. Put-in next to Cotton Volunteer Fire Department, down a steep bank. Another steep bank at the take-out.

(2) NC 87 bridge to Huske Lock on the Cape Fear River

Drop: 6′	**Time:** 7 hrs.
Difficulty: A	**Scenery:** B
Distance: 15 mi.	**Water Quality:** Fair

Gauge: Runnable year round.

Difficulties: Downed trees, snags. There are 2 miles on the Rockfish, then 13 on the Cape Fear to the first practical take-out at Huske Lock, located just down into Bladen County and accessible from Bladen County Rt. 1304, the first turn off NC 87. (See Cape Fear River, section 6.) Fishing boats are common on the Cape Fear. This trip could be done as a camper.

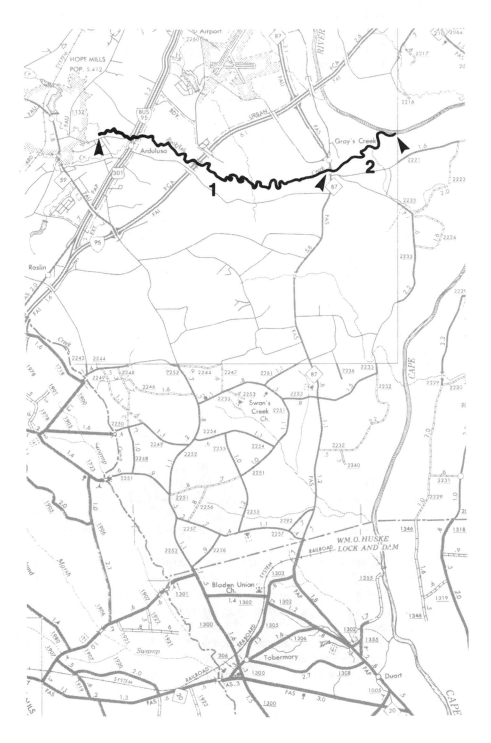

Rocky River

This Rocky River, not to be confused with many others of the same name, is a tributary of the Deep, with which it merges a few miles above US 1. It would be a most popular whitewater run except that it drains a small area nestled between the Deep and the Haw; thus it is only canoeable in wet weather. Unfortunately, it is also polluted by Siler City sewage.

Topo Maps: Colon, Pittsboro, Siler City NE, Siler City

County: Chatham

(1) US 64 bridge near Siler City to Chatham County Rt. 2156

Drop: 180′
Difficulty: 1-2-3/4
Distance: 16 mi.

Time: 5 hrs.
Scenery: A-B
Water Quality: Fair

Gauge: On Rt. 902 bridge; "0" is minimum for solo paddling.

Difficulties: The best whitewater is located in the six miles below Rt. 2170 bridge, where some technical rock gardens can be Class 4 at high water. There are remains of at least five stone dams in this section, all of which can be run. The last mile is flatwater backed up by the 20-foot hydro dam at the take-out.

(2) Chatham County Rt. 2156 to US 1 bridge over the Deep River

Drop: 110′
Difficulty: 1-2-3
Distance: 9.6 mi.

Time: 3.5 hrs.
Scenery: A-B
Water Quality: Fair

Gauge: At Rt. 1953 bridge, which can serve as an alternate put-in.

Difficulties: There are two major sets of rapids. The first starts a half mile below Rt. 1953 bridge and terminates with a three-foot ledge within sight of US 15-501 bridge. The second set begins a mile later and is more constricted than the first, reaching Class 3 difficulty at higher water levels. Scouting from the rocks is advised.

There is no access at the confluence with the Deep, so continue four miles to US 1 bridge for the take-out. Just above the take-out is a large dam which is perhaps the most difficult portage in the East. The left generally is badly obstructed by debris; the right is preferred. Lift up the cliff, carry a short distance along the edge, then drop the boat down 60 feet to relaunch below the dam. *Do not* enter the millrace on the left because water flows through the wheelhouse, creating a death trap. Take-out is easiest on the right just below the bridge.

Osprey nest along the Lockwood Folly River

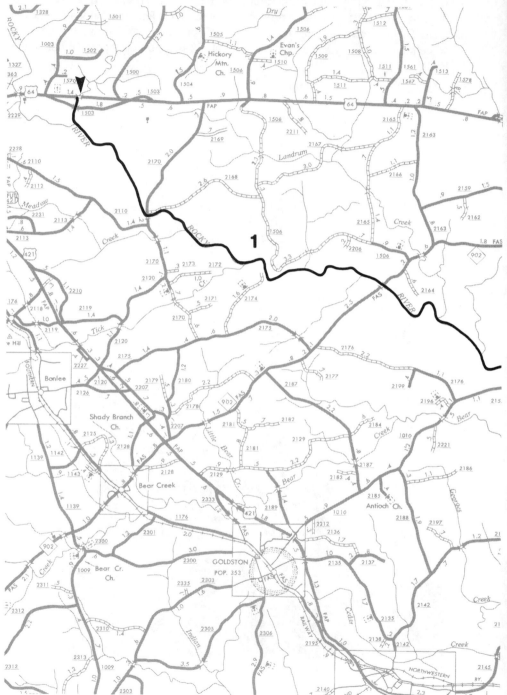

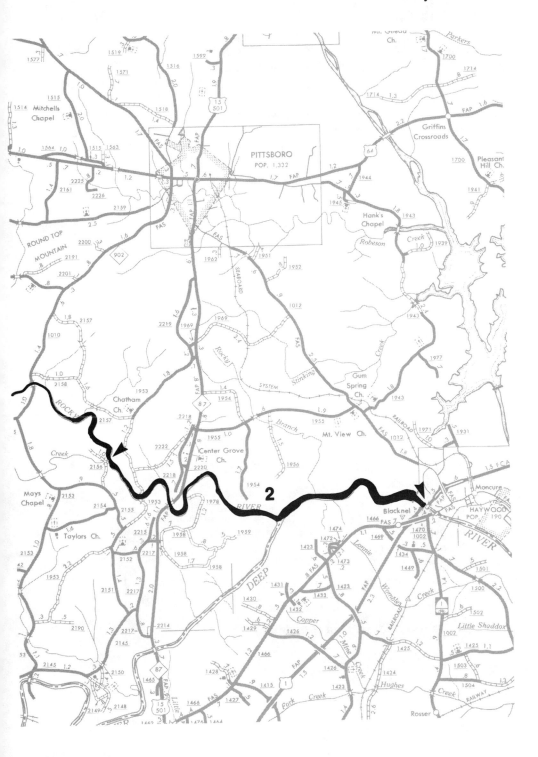

South River

The South River heads up in the vicinity of Angier in northeast Harnett County as the Black River. It becomes known as the South below the confluence of Mingo Swamp south of Dunn. The river flows to the south and east to its confluence with the Black down from Ivanhoe.

In 1784 when Sampson County was chopped off from Duplin County, the entire river was called the Black. But since Sampson already had a Black River, it was decided it did not need two, especially two so closely located. The eastern stream become South Black River, and finally, just the plain South.

The South is a slow-moving black water swamp stream with fairly low banks except for an occasional high bluff.

Topo Maps: Garland, Whitelake

Counties: Bladen, Sampson

(1) Wildlife access area at US 701 bridge (Sloans Bridge) to NC 41 bridge

Drop: 10′	**Time:** 3.5 hrs.
Difficulty: B	**Scenery:** A
Distance: 8.2 mi.	**Water Quality:** Good

Gauge: USGS gauge at NC 41 bridge. Runnable generally during wet seasons.

Difficulties: None, except possible downed trees.

(2) NC 41 bridge to wildlife access area at Bladen County Rt. 1007 bridge (Ennis Bridge)

Drop: 8′	**Time:** 3.5 hrs.
Difficulty: B	**Scenery:** A
Distance: 8.6 mi.	**Water Quality:** Good

Gauge: USGS gauge at NC 41 bridge. Runnable generally during wet seasons.

Difficulties: None, except possible downed trees.

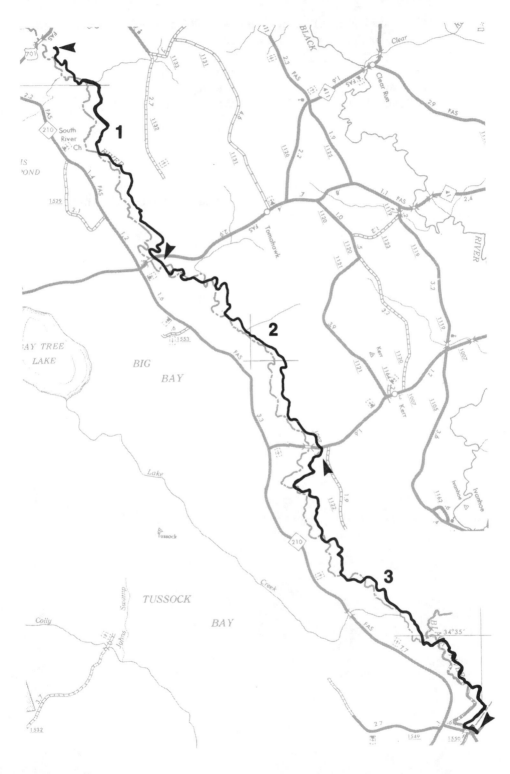

(3) Wildlife access area at Bladen County Rt. 1007 bridge (Ennis Bridge) to Rt. 1550 bridge over the Black River

Drop: 12 ′   **Time:** 4.5 hrs.
Difficulty: B   **Scenery:** A
Distance: 11.8 mi.   **Water Quality:** Good

Gauge: USGS gauge at NC 41 bridge. Runnable except during dry seasons.

Difficulties: None.

The river confluences with the Black about eight miles below the put-in. Refer to the Black River for further information.

Town Creek

Town Creek heads up in the Little Green Swamp in Brunswick County and flows generally east to the Cape Fear River down from Wilmington. It begins as a typical black water stream in primarily swamp terrain and ends up more brackish as it completes its course through the marshes.

Topo Maps: Winnabow, Wilmington

County: Brunswick

(1) US 17 bridge north of creek bridge to NC 133 bridge

Drop: 0'
Difficulty: A
Distance: 16.8 mi.

Time: 6.5-7 hrs.
Scenery: A
Water Quality: Good

Gauge: None. Runnable year round.

Difficulties: None. Passage is wide and open and quite evident with one exception. About two miles from the put-in, just beyond trailers on the left, bear right. The main course appears to be straight. Tides can be a factor in paddling time in the last few miles.

A number of areas with high ground suitable for camping are interspersed along the first half of this section. This is all private property, much of it leased by hunting clubs, so it is best to obtain permission for camping.

(2) NC 133 bridge to Cape Fear River and return

Drop: 0'
Difficulty: A-B
Distance: 8 mi.

Time: 3.5 hrs.
Scenery: A
Water Quality: Good

Gauge: None. Runnable year round.

Difficulties: This section is tidal, and the only difficulties should result from the tides. Timing trips to coincide with the outgoing and incoming tides will make for a much easier trip.

A visit to Campbell Island on the Cape Fear will make for a more interesting trip, but it can add a couple of miles as well as additional paddling time to your trip.

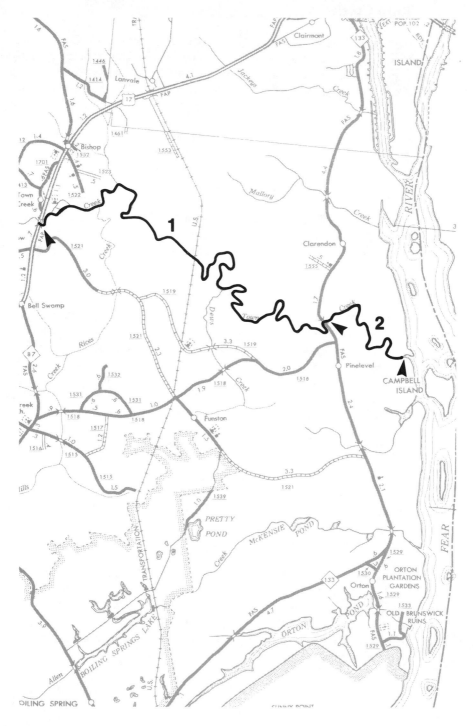

Upper Little River

Formed in western Harnett County and flowing easterly to the Cape Fear, the Upper Little River is a scenic small stream suitable for paddling when other rivers are high or for an easy trip in cold weather. Holly and mistletoe in thick profusion make this a particularly nice Christmas cruise. Varying in width from 30 to 50 feet, it flows briskly at three to five miles per hour. The water is normally a clear tea color.

Topo Maps: Bunn Level, Erwin

County: Harnett

Between US 401 and Harnett County Rt. 2016, the river flows through swamp and lowland woods containing many snags and downed trees. In places the channel is not well defined. It can be explored by canoe only in high water by those willing to tackle the difficulties.

(1) Harnett County Rt. 2016 bridge to the Cape Fear River, NC 217 bridge

Drop: 48′
Difficulty: C-1-2
Distance: 8 mi.

Time: 3.5 hrs.
Scenery: A
Water Quality: Good

Gauge: On bridge piling at Rt. 2016. Can be done over a wide range from below 0 to over 3′ with little change in difficulty. Too low only after a prolonged dry spell.

Difficulties: Snags, downed trees, low branches. Fast water around bends will be difficult for beginners. In the last one and a half miles the river drops over a series of ten low ledges to reach bedrock at the level of the Cape Fear. After reaching the Cape Fear, there remains one mile on the much larger river and one difficult rapid. See Cape Fear, section 3, for description.

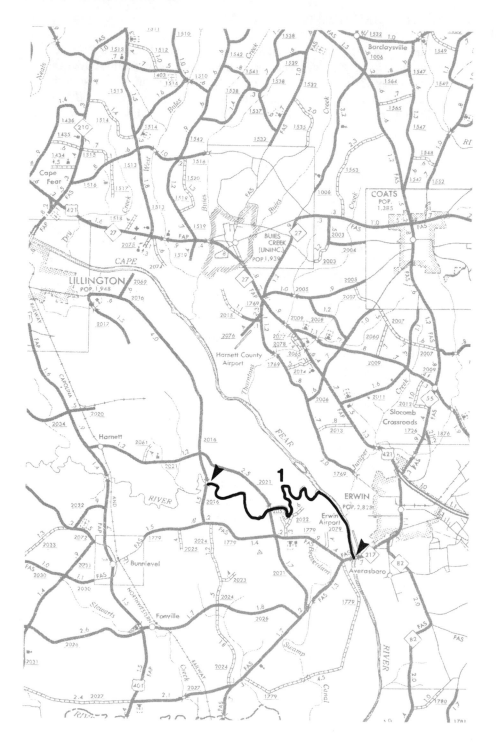

3
Roanoke Basin

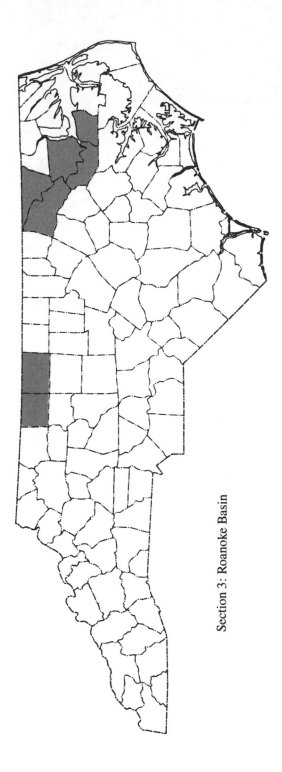

Section 3: Roanoke Basin

Dan River

The Dan River flows off the crest of the Blue Ridge beneath the Pinnacles of Dan, where it is piped down the mountains through the turbines of the City of Danville Power Plant above the community of Kibler. From the power plant it wanders southeast through hills of laurel and rhododendron before turning northeast and entering Virginia east of Eden. It then flows generally east until it confluences with the Roanoke River.

The Dan was named after Danaho, a Saura Indian chief. The Saura Indians lived along the river, with upper Saura Town situated near the junction of the Smith and Dan and lower Saura Town located near the former town of Draper.

As one paddles the upper sections in North Carolina, to the south he will catch glimpses of the Sauratown Mountains, one of the most easterly mountainous areas in the state, where Hanging Rock State Park is located. The park consists of rugged mountain terrain and has excellent camping facilities.

Topo Maps: Claudville, Stuart S.E. VA; Hanging Rock, Danbury, Ayersville, Belews Lake, Walnut Cove, Mayodan, South West Eden, South East Eden, Draper, NC-VA; Brosville, NC-VA

Counties: Patrick, VA; Stokes, Rockingham, NC

(1) City of Danville Power Plant at Kibler to Patrick County Rt. 773 bridge

Drop: 225′
Difficulty: 1-2-3
Distance: 8 mi.

Time: 3.5 hrs.
Scenery: B
Water Quality: Excellent

Gauge: None. To check on the water flow, call Pinnacles Hydroelectric Station, (703) 251-5141, and ask for the water flow. A minimum would be 5,600 k.w. Maximum possible flow is 9,600, at which open canoes can run safely.

Difficulties: The first half mile below the put-in drops very fast. About 200 yards below the first bridge, a three-foot drop pushes much of the water into a large boulder on the right. If entered too far to the right, much of the boat is also pushed against the boulder. This rock is undercut, so be very cautious in trying to dislodge a broached canoe.

A very low-water bridge is located around the bend to the right, about two miles below the power plant. Stay close to the right.

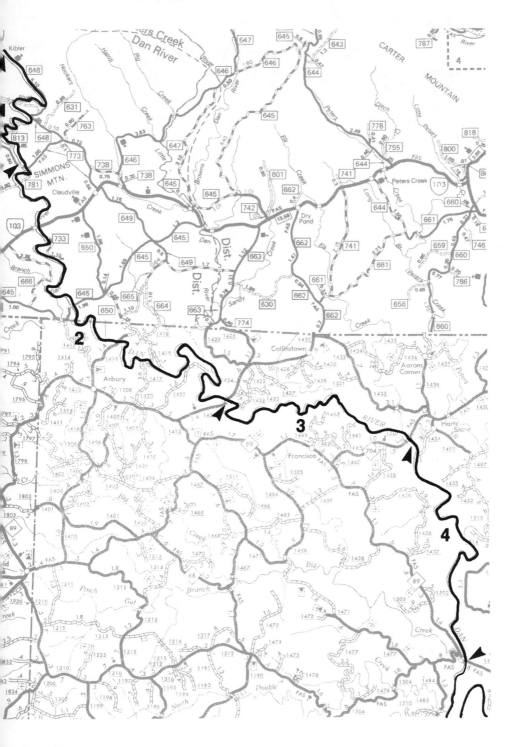

(2) Patrick County Rt. 773 bridge to Stokes County Rt. 1432 bridge (Collinstown Road) at Jessups Mill

> **Drop:** 224′
> **Difficulty:** 1-2/3
> **Distance:** 12.5 mi.
>
> **Time:** 5.5 hrs.
> **Scenery:** A
> **Water Quality:** Good

Gauge: USGS gauge located 75 feet above NC 704 bridge on the north bank. A reading of 1.7 is minimum for solo, or phone Pinnacles Hydroelectric Station (see section 1) for a reading (5,600 k.w. minimum).

Difficulties: Primarily fast water approaches through small rock gardens and over small ledges. Following the second bridge (Stokes County Rt. 1416) below VA 103 bridge, a series of ledges ends in a Class 3, requiring an S turn. Scout on the left. Stokes County Rt. 1417, Joyce Mill Road, is immediately below these rapids.

(3) Stokes County Rt. 1432 bridge (Collinstown Road) at Jessups Mill to NC 704 bridge (Clements Ford)

> **Drop:** 128′
> **Difficulty:** 1-2
> **Distance:** 8.5 mi.
>
> **Time:** 4 hrs.
> **Scenery:** A
> **Water Quality:** Good

Gauge: USGS gauge is 1.7 minimum for solo.

Difficulties: One rapid where the river drops abruptly over a bed of rocks and narrows between two large boulders. Easily recognizable. An excellent lunch stop.

(4) NC 704 bridge to NC 89 bridge

> **Drop:** 72′
> **Difficulty:** 1-2
> **Distance:** 7 mi.
>
> **Time:** 3 hrs.
> **Scenery:** A
> **Water Quality:** Good

Gauge: USGS gauge is 1.55 minimum for solo.

Difficulties: Many small gravel bars at lower water levels.

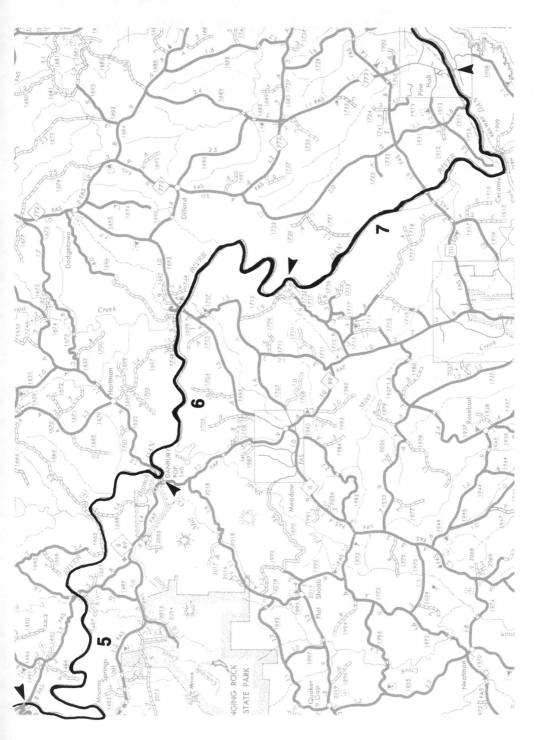

(5) NC 89 bridge (Clements Ford) to Stokes County Rt. 1652 bridge at Danbury

Drop: 70′
Difficulty: 1-2
Distance: 10.5 mi.

Time: 5 hrs.
Scenery: A-B
Water Quality: Good

Gauge: USGS gauge is 1.55 minimum for solo.

Difficulties: None, except one sharply undercut bank in a sharp bend to the left, just below the put-in. Below the second bridge after NC 89, be on the lookout for some caves in the cliff on the right. The more ambitious may be tempted to climb to them. The difficulties here are the great clusters of poison ivy growing in the entrance.

(6) Stokes County Rt. 1652 bridge at Danbury to end of Rt. 1712 (below washed-out dam)

Drop: 53′
Difficulty: 1-2
Distance: 8.8 mi.

Time: 3.5 hrs.
Scenery: A
Water Quality: Good

Gauge: Runnable year round except during dry seasons.

Difficulties: The remains of a dynamited dam just above the take-out could prove dangerous. Easily scouted from the right bank. If questionable, pull out for a short carry to the take-out.

(7) End of Stokes County Rt. 1712 (below washed-out dam) to NC 772 bridge in Pine Hall

Drop: 51′
Difficulty: 1-2
Distance: 9 mi.

Time: 3.5 hrs.
Scenery: A
Water Quality: Good

Gauge: Runnable year round except during dry seasons.

Difficulties: Shoals above island. Best run on the left.

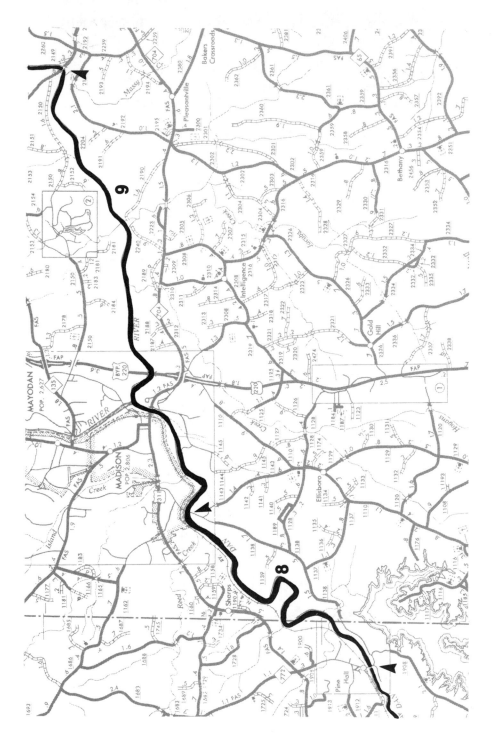

(8) NC 772 bridge in Pine Hall to Rockingham County Rt. 1138 bridge (Lindsay Bridge Road)

Drop: 37′
Difficulty: 1
Distance: 6.5 mi.

Time: 2.5 hrs.
Scenery: B-C
Water Quality: Good

Gauge: Runnable year round except during dry seasons.

Difficulties: A six-foot dam located just above 1138 bridge and opposite the brickyard can best be carried on the right (40-yard carry).

(9) Rockingham County Rt. 1138 bridge (Lindsay Bridge Road) to Rt. 2150 bridge.

Drop: 42′
Difficulty: C-1
Distance: 10.8 mi.

Time: 3.5 hrs.
Scenery: B-C
Water Quality: Fair

Gauge: Runnable year round.

Difficulties: None except a series of small washed-out dams downstream from US 220 bridge. They extend for some 100 yards with steel rods exposed; the center, however, is clear.

(10) Rockingham County Rt. 2150 bridge to wildlife access area off Rt. 2039 south of Leakesville

Drop: 21′
Difficulty: 1-2
Distance: 11.5 mi.

Time: 4 hrs.
Scenery: A-B
Water Quality: Fair

Gauge: USGS gauge 100 yards downstream on right. Minimum for solo is a reading of 1.50.

Difficulties: None.

(11) Wildlife access area off Rockingham County Rt. 2039 south of Leakesville to Rt. 1761 bridge (VA Rt. 880) at Virginia state line

Drop: 29′
Difficulty: C-1
Distance: 10.6 mi.

Time: 4 hrs.
Scenery: A-B
Water Quality: Fair

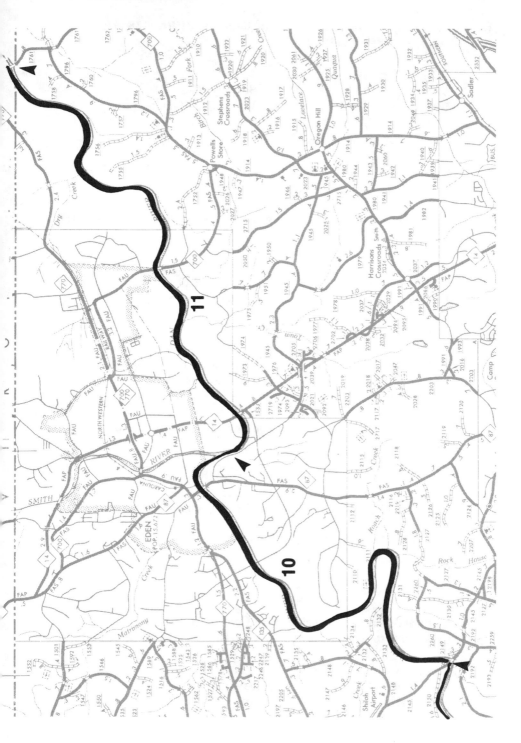

Gauge: Runnable all year except during extremely dry seasons.

Difficulties: A six-foot-high dam located one and two-tenths miles downstream from NC 14 bridge has a fairly strong hydraulic. A short carry on the right will be necessary.

Roanoke River

The Roanoke River heads up on the eastern slopes of the Allegheny Mountains, cuts through the Blue Ridge, and becomes the Staunton on its journey across Virginia until it reaches the Dan at Kerr Reservoir, where it takes on its original name again. It then continues on into North Carolina through Lake Gaston and Roanoke Rapids Lake below the dam to where we begin our journey toward Albemarle Sound.

The town of Roanoke Rapids was originally known as Great Falls, and it was to this vicinity that the earliest travel of white man was reported. Ralph Lane traveled from Fort Raleigh on Roanoke Island to the rocks and falls around Weldon in 1586.

Halifax was a port of call around 1750, and steamboat traffic flourished as far up as Weldon Place until 1845. Halifax has a historical district which is well worth a visit. A canal with locks, begun in 1819 and completed in 1834, ran for almost eight miles between Weldon and Great Falls and was in use until 1859 when the railroad began to take over. Remains of the locks can still be found and are on the National Register of historic places.

The Roanoke has the widest floodplain, five miles, of any river in the state. As a result of this feature and extensive land clearing, heavy flooding has caused great damage, as in 1877 when the river rose 50 feet and in August 1940 when it rose 57 feet, which resulted in the construction of Briggs Island Dam. This widespread flooding forced many of the oldest towns such as Halifax and Scotland Neck, originally located on the river, to relocate on higher ground.

The river makes big bends as it snakes its way slowly to Albemarle Sound through some of the most secluded land in eastern North Carolina. The terrain varies between swampland on the one side and high bluffs, looming occasionally, on the other.

Volume can vary greatly in the upper sections as a result of water releases from the dam. Great care should be taken through this area.

Topo Maps: Roanoke Rapids, Weldon, Halifax, Boones Crossroads, Scotland Neck, Norfleet, Palmyra, Woodville, Hamilton, Quitsna, Williamston, Jamesville, Windsor South, Plymouth West, Woodard, Plymouth East, Westover.

Counties: Northampton, Halifax, Bertie, Martin, Washington

(1) NC 48 bridge at Roanoke Rapids to the wildlife access area at US 301 bridge in Weldon

Drop: 15′	**Time:** 2.5 hrs.
Difficulty: 1-2	**Scenery:** B-C
Distance: 5.6 mi.	**Water Quality:** Poor

148

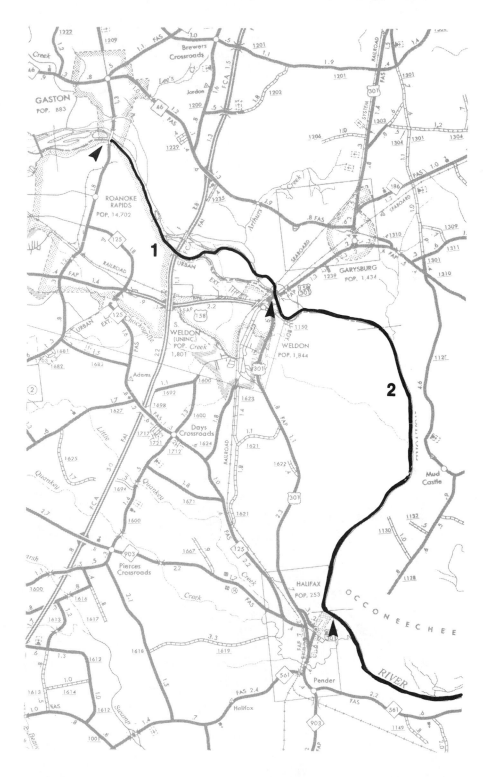

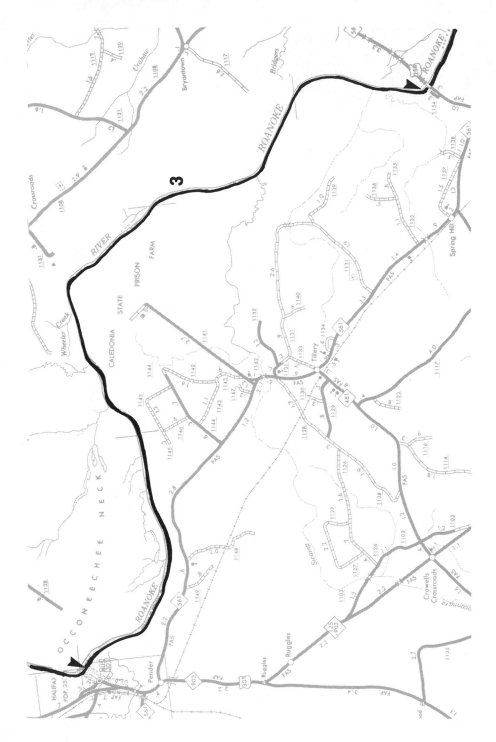

Gauge: Can be paddled year round.

Difficulties: Beware of the great fluctuations in water flow through the rock gardens when water is released from the dam.

The lower portion of the run is heavily fished during the spring spawning of rockfish (striped bass). For this reason the powerboat traffic will increase a lot during this time.

(2) Wildlife access area at US 301 bridge in Weldon to the outskirts of Halifax

Drop: 17′	**Time:** 4 hrs.
Difficulty: C-1	**Scenery:** A-B
Distance: 9.3 mi.	**Water Quality:** Poor-Fair

Gauge: Can be paddled year round.

Difficulties: A horseshoe ledge dropping about four feet, just downstream from the put-in, can present a keeper on the far right at certain water levels. When a full release is being made, this ledge is mostly washed out.

(3) Halifax to US 258 bridge north of Scotland Neck

Drop: 9′	**Time:** 6-7.5 hrs.
Difficulty: B	**Scenery:** A
Distance: 19 mi.	**Water Quality:** Fair

Gauge: None. Can be run all year.

Difficulties: None; however, extra precautions should be taken to select high-ground campsites since upstream releases can cause the water level to fluctuate substantially.

Caledonia State Prison lies on the south side of the river in the big bend below Occoneechee Neck, so a campsite selection on the north bank might make one sleep a bit more peacefully.

(4) US 258 bridge north of Scotland Neck to NC 11 bridge

Drop: 10′	**Time:** 9-10 hrs.
Difficulty: B	**Scenery:** A
Distance: 26.5 mi.	**Water Quality:** Fair

Gauge: None. Can be run all year.

Difficulties: None.

(5) NC 11 bridge to the wildlife access area at Hamilton

Drop: 4 ′   **Time:** 5 hrs.
Difficulty: B   **Scenery:** A
Distance: 11 mi.   **Water Quality:** Fair-Good

Gauge: None. Can be run all year.

Difficulties: None.
Broadneck Swamp is on the north side of the river and runs for some distance.

Beaver dam on Merchants Mill Pond

(6) Wildlife access area at Hamilton to US 13-17 bridge at Williamston

Drop: 5′   **Time:** 9-10 hrs.
Difficulty: A-B   **Scenery:** A
Distance: 23 mi.   **Water Quality:** Good

Gauge: None. Can be run all year.

Difficulties: None. The upper few miles stretch through lowland swamps, which are located mostly on the north side.

(7) US 13-17 bridge at Williamston to outskirts of Jamesville

Drop: 5′   **Time:** 6-7 hrs.
Difficulty: A-B   **Scenery:** A
Distance: 17 mi.   **Water Quality:** Good

Gauge: None. Can be run all year.

Difficulties: None.

(8) Jamesville to wildlife access area at NC 45 bridge east of Plymouth

Drop: 0′   **Time:** 6-7 hrs.
Difficulty: A-B   **Scenery:** A
Distance: 15.3 mi.   **Water Quality:** Good

Gauge: None. Runnable year round.

Difficulties: None, except winds and tides that can create problems when estimating travel time.

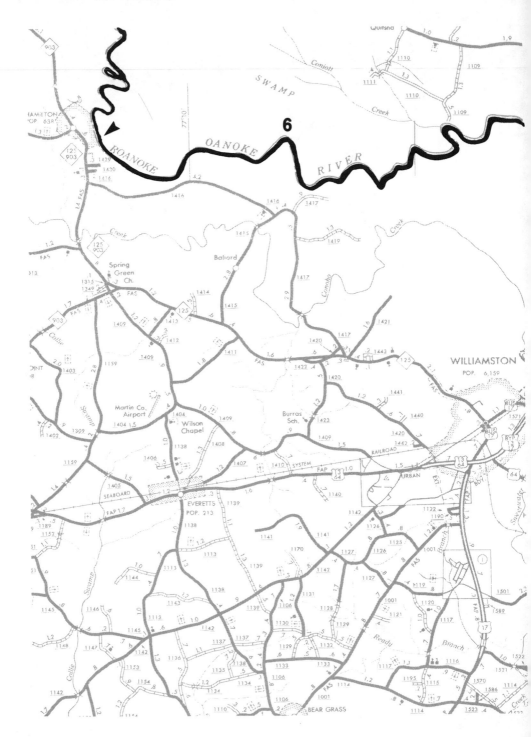

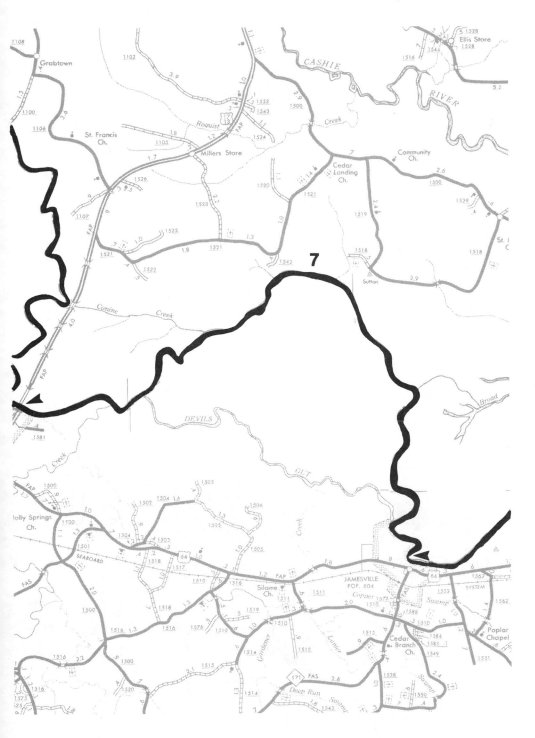

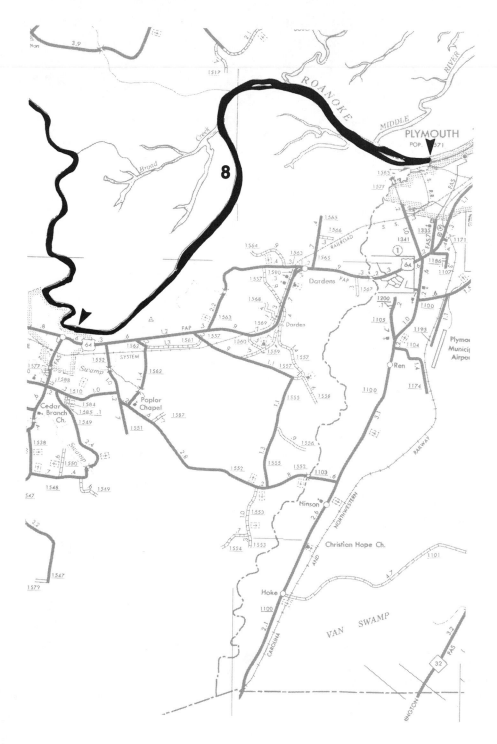

Snow Creek

Snow Creek* flows southward into the Dan River a few miles below Danbury. A relatively small stream, it often has adequate depth in the section indicated, particularly in the spring and following rains. It flows through a narrow valley with many exposed rock formations and is comparable to the upper Dan in character and attractiveness.

Topo Map: Danbury

County: Stokes

(1) Stokes County Rt. 1674 bridge to Rt. 1695 bridge across the Dan, 0.2 miles below the confluence

Drop: 50′	**Time:** 2 hrs.
Difficulty: 1-2/3	**Scenery:** A
Distance: 4.9 mi.	**Water Quality:** Good

Gauge: At Rt. 1674 bridge. Minimum for solo is 2″ below 0. Can usually be run in spring and following rains.

Difficulties: Overhanging branches and possible fallen trees. About a mile above the creek mouth, the whole stream flows through a crevice about three feet wide at lower levels, which needs to be scouted. Easy to scout and portage on left.

---

*From the notes of Allen Trelease.

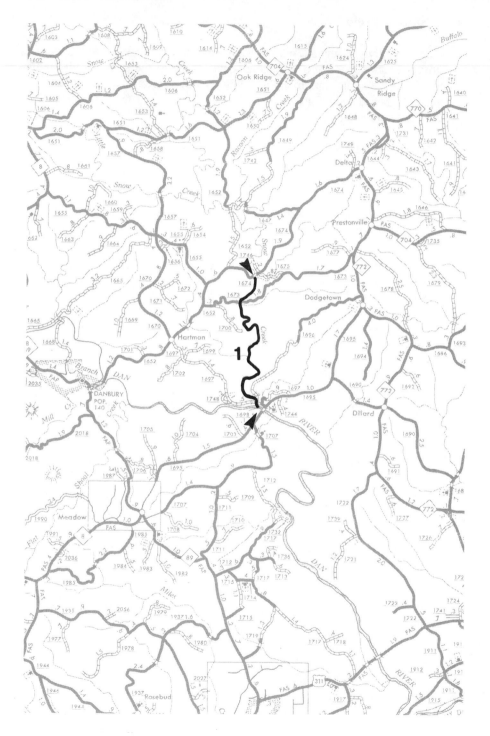

4

Tar–Pamlico Basin

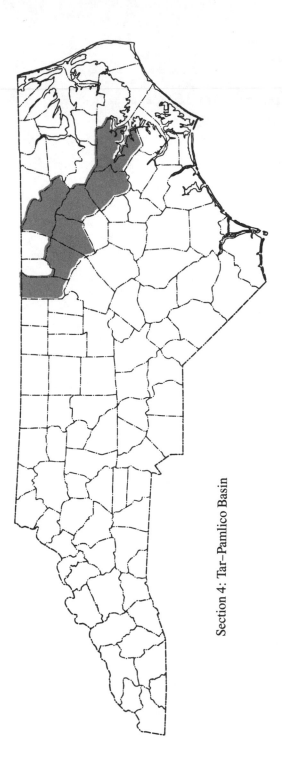

Section 4: Tar–Pamlico Basin

Chicod Creek

Chicod Creek received national attention in the 1960s and 1970s when plans to channelize it were contested in the courts by conservationists. As a result of litigation, the creek has remained unchannelized, but it has been "dragged free" of major snags and fallen obstacles. Since the early 1980s, its shores have undergone relatively rapid development, but Chicod Creek still offers a pleasant variety of sections--ranging from "The Narrows," where after-rain waters run fast, to the broader and deeper depths that still embrace at least one sunken ship of Civil War vintage.

Topo Map: Chocowinity

County: Pitt

(1) NC 33 bridge to "Seine Beach" at Pitt County Rt. 1565

Drop: 0′   **Time:** 1.5 hrs.
Difficulty: A   **Scenery:** B
Distance: 3 mi.   **Water Quality:** Fair

Gauge: None.

Difficulties: Primarily underwater objects that may present a hazard to thin-hulled crafts.

The short distance and slow-moving water, combined with the necessity of using the commercial site at "Seine Beach," are conducive to paddling round trip, which will normally be a casual half-day trip.

The property off the south side of NC 33 at the put-in is "most definitely private" land so it is best not to go wandering.

Directions: *Put-in*--Bridge one mile west of Grimesland Park on the south side of road, or park and launch on north side for a small fee.

Take-out--"Seine Beach," a small commercial landing on the Tar River a few hundred yards from the junction of Chicod Creek and the Tar. Rt. 1565 bridge is approximately one mile north of Grimesland.

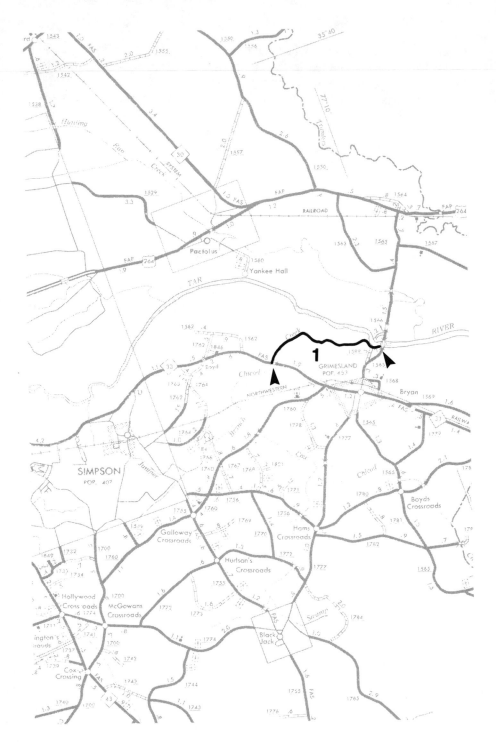

Fishing Creek

Fishing Creek, the largest tributary of the Tar River, springs up a few miles west of Warrenton in Warren County and twists its way southeasterly to form the line between Nash and Halifax counties. It then turns south into Edgecombe County to meet the Tar just north of Tarboro. The creek, relatively unspoiled, makes its way through the fall line quite gradually, thereby creating few drops of any significance. It is quite isolated along the entire course.

Topo Maps: Essex, Ringwood, Enfield, Whitakers, Draughn, Tarboro (15 min.)

Counties: Halifax, Edgecombe

(1) Halifax County Rt. 1327 bridge to NC 48 bridge

Drop: 18′   **Time:** 3.75 hrs.
Difficulty: 1   **Scenery:** A-B
Distance: 9.8 mi.   **Water Quality:** Fair

Gauge: USGS gauge at US 301 bridge. A reading under 3.2 should be considered minimum.

Difficulties: There is a small shoals at about the eight-mile point. Just below, the remnants of an old dam can best be run on the left. The possibility of encountering downed trees is ever present.

(2) NC 48 bridge to US 301 bridge

Drop: 12′   **Time:** 3.5 hrs.
Difficulty: B   **Scenery:** A
Distance: 9.1 mi.   **Water Quality:** Fair

Gauge: USGS gauge at US 301 bridge. A reading of 3.0 should be considered a minimum.

Difficulties: Bellamy Mill Dam, about eight feet high, is approximately three miles below I-95 (100 yards above Nash County 1518 bridge). It can best be carried on the right. Also possible downed trees, especially below the power line clearings.

There is an exceptionally nice bald cypress specimen a few minutes below 1518 bridge.

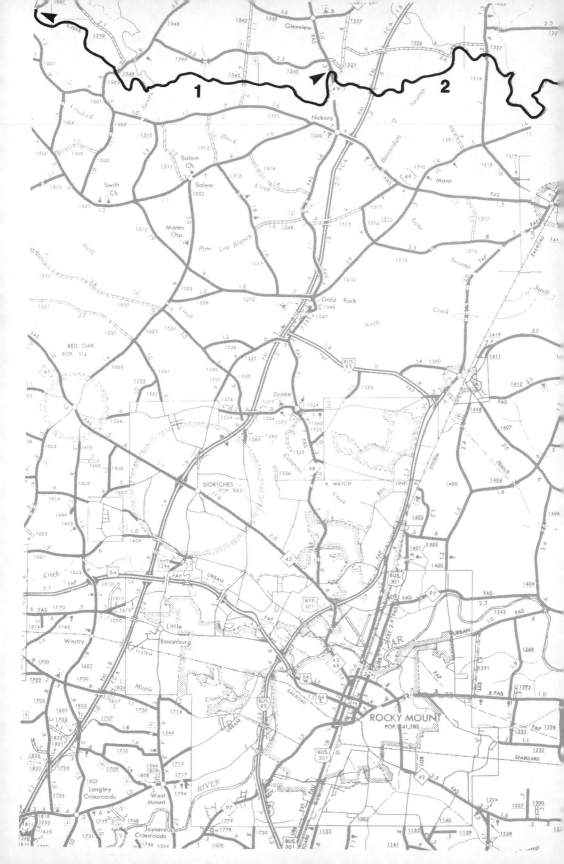

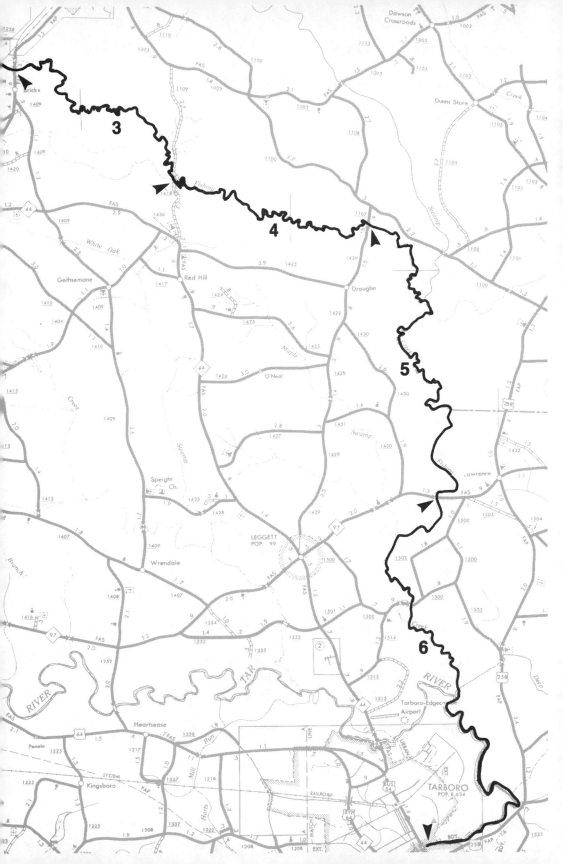

(3) US 301 bridge to Edgecombe County Rt. 1418 bridge

Drop: 13'   **Time:** 4.5 hrs.
Difficulty: B   **Scenery:** A
Distance: 9.9 mi.   **Water Quality:** Fair

Gauge: US 301 gauge. A reading of 2.5 should be considered a minimum.

Difficulties: A good possibility of several downed trees. Approach with caution at higher water levels.

(4) Edgecombe County Rt. 1418 bridge to Rt. 1429 bridge

Drop: 20'   **Time:** 4.15 hrs.
Difficulty: B   **Scenery:** A
Distance: 10.5 mi.   **Water Quality:** Fair

Gauge: US 301 gauge. A reading of 2.4 should be considered a minimum.

Difficulties: Downed trees.

(5) Edgecombe County Rt. 1429 bridge to NC 97 bridge

Drop: 11'   **Time:** 6 hrs.
Difficulty: B   **Scenery:** A
Distance: 14.6 mi.   **Water Quality:** Fair

Gauge: Generally runnable year round except following extremely dry spells.

Difficulties: Downed trees.

(6) NC 97 bridge to US 64 bridge on the Tar (Riverfront Park) in Tarboro

Drop: 29'   **Time:** 6 hrs.
Difficulty: A-B   **Scenery:** A-B
Distance: 14.2 mi.   **Water Quality:** Fair

Gauge: Generally runnable year round except following extremely dry spells.

Difficulties: Downed trees.

Little Fishing Creek

This small Tar River tributary heads up near Oxford, in Granville County, and flows southeasterly to merge with the Tar just at Rt. 1622 bridge. Runnable only during times of high water, Little Fishing Creek winds around scenic wooded hills and through some pastureland. About a half mile below the put-in, the volume doubles with the addition of Coon Creek.

Topo Map: Oxford

County: Granville

(1) NC 96 bridge to Granville County Rt. 1622 over the Tar

Drop: 60′   **Time:** 3 hrs.
Difficulty: C-1-2   **Scenery:** A-B
Distance: 7 mi.   **Water Quality:** Fair

Gauge: USGS gauge 100 feet above NC 96 bridge on the right. Minimum reading of 4.0 for a good run.

Difficulties: A good possibility of logjams, so beware. A Class 2 is located just below Rt. 1643 bridge.

For a map of Little Fishing Creek, see pages 172–73.

Tar River

The city of Roxboro, in Person County, sits atop the high ground that is a major divide in the Piedmont. To the north of town, creeks flow to the Roanoke, to the south is the Flat at the head of the Neuse basin, and to the east lie the headwaters of the Tar River. The countryside along the upper miles of the Tar is still rural; the old streamside mills and dams have been washed away. If any river in the Piedmont qualifies for special protection as a scenic river, then certainly the upper portion of the Tar does.

From the hills the river winds its way south and east across the Piedmont before making a final drop through the fall line at Rocky Mount. It then turns into the Coastal Plain and beyond Greenville empties into the Pamlico River.

The most important native product of the early days of settlement was tar, and it is believed that the river derived its name because of the product. The river was heavily used for transportation in the eighties and nineties as steamboats regularly plied between Washington and Tarboro. Although used for trading since early times, the river was evidently widely used also as a recreational resource with most families owning a boat of some sort. Apparently canoes were quite common also.

A note of interest for UNC fans. Legend has it that Cornwallis's soldiers, while fording the river near Rocky Mount, found their feet blackened by the tar that had been dumped into the river. They announced, cursing, that "anyone will get 'tar heels' if they wade the streams of this state." (Perhaps we can give the State fans equal time elsewhere.)

Topo Maps: Berea, Stem, Wilton, Kittrell, Ingleside, Louisburg, Justice, Bunn East, Spring Hope, Bailey, Winstead Crossroads, Nashville, Rocky Mount, Hartsease, Tarboro, Speed, Old Sparta, Falkland, Greenville NW and SW

Counties: Granville, Franklin, Nash, Edgecombe, Pitt

Above Granville County Rt. 1004, the Tar is very small with many trees down across the river. There is a four-foot dam about one mile above Rt. 1004 where the city of Oxford draws its water supply.

(1) Granville County Rt. 1004 bridge to NC 15 bridge

Drop: 58′	**Time:** 2.5 hrs.
Difficulty: 1-2	**Scenery:** A
Distance: 4.2 mi.	**Water Quality:** Good

Gauge: Painted on 1004 bridge. The 0 is minimum for solo paddling. Primarily runnable during wet weather.

Difficulties: Several washed-out dams should be watched for. Rock gardens above and below the railroad bridge as well as near the two other bridges.

(2) NC 15 bridge to NC 96 bridge

Drop: 9′
Difficulty: B
Distance: 4.2 mi.

Time: 2.5 hrs.
Scenery: B
Water Quality: Good

Gauge: USGS gauge 100 feet above NC 96 bridge on the right. Minimum for solo is 2.5. Generally runnable all year.

Difficulties: None, except downed trees.

(3) NC 96 bridge to Franklin County Rt. 1203 bridge at the county line

Drop: 80′
Difficulty: 1-2+
Distance: 5.9 mi.

Time: 3 hrs.
Scenery: AA
Water Quality: Good

Gauge: See section 2 for location. Just below the gauge is a "sharp-notched weir" that causes water levels to stabilize near 2.5. An absolute minimum for solo is 2.7. Generally runnable in wet weather.

Difficulties: The river divides into as many as five channels through the numerous small islands, so beware of debris-clogged passages and strainers. At the five-mile point the channel narrows appreciably and is split by a rock. Approach cautiously at higher water levels.

(4) Franklin County Rt. 1203 bridge at the county line to Rt. 1003 bridge

Drop: 24′
Difficulty: B
Distance: 12.9 mi.

Time: 6 hrs.
Scenery: B
Water Quality: Good

Gauge: See section 2. Minimum for solo is 2.2. Runnable except following dry spells.

Difficulties: Generally a fair amount of timber is down across the streambed.

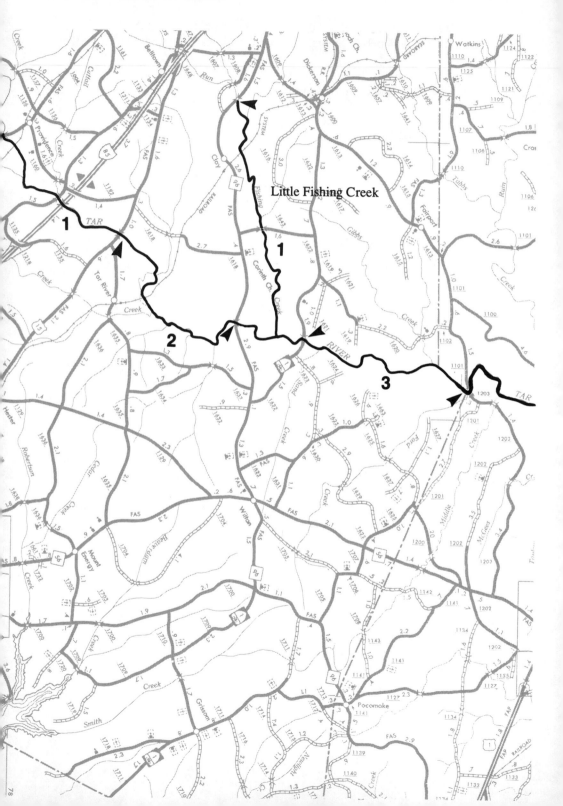

(5) Franklin County Rt. 1003 bridge to US 401 bridge in Louisburg

Drop: 16′
Difficulty: B
Distance: 8.5 mi.

Time: 4 hrs.
Scenery: B
Water Quality: Good

Gauge: USGS gauge at NC 96 bridge. Minimum for solo is 2.2. Runnable except after a prolonged dry spell.

Difficulties: Downed trees. About one mile above Louisburg, a small dam with a water-intake tower might require a carry-over at lower water levels. Then within sight of the Main Street Bridge are the remains of an old stone mill dam. It is washed out on the right side and presents a few standing waves.

(6) US 401 bridge in Louisburg to Franklin County Rt. 1001 bridge

Drop: 20′
Difficulty: B
Distance: 10.6 mi.

Time: 5 hrs.
Scenery: B-C
Water Quality: Fair

Gauge: USGS gauge at NC 96 bridge. Minimum for solo is 2.4.

Difficulties: Runnable except following a long dry spell. Downed trees make passage difficult at lower water levels.

(7) Franklin County Rt. 1001 bridge to end of Nash County Rt. 1331 at Webb's Mill

Drop: 18′
Difficulty: B-1
Distance: 10.5 mi.

Time: 4.5 hrs.
Scenery: A
Water Quality: Fair

Gauge: Runnable year round.

Difficulties: None, except a few riffles. Approach the dam at Webb's Mill on the left side and carry on the left. At lower water levels one may enter the mill run and take out. At higher levels, take out under the old bridge for a longer but safer move.

(8) Nash County Rt. 1331 at Webb's Mill to NC 581 bridge

Drop: 16′
Difficulty: B
Distance: 6.4 mi.

Time: 2.5 hrs.
Scenery: A
Water Quality: Fair

Gauge: Runnable year round.

Difficulties: None.

(9) NC 581 bridge to Nash County Rt. 1981 bridge

Drop: 9′   **Time:** 4 hrs.
Difficulty: B   **Scenery:** A
Distance: 9.2 mi.   **Water Quality:** Fair

Gauge: Runnable year round.

Difficulties: None.

(10) Nash County Rt. 1981 bridge to dam at end of Rt. 1746

Drop: 0′   **Time:** 4 hrs.
Difficulty: A   **Scenery:** A-B-C
Distance: 8.2 mi.   **Water Quality:** Fair

Gauge: Runnable year round.

Difficulties: Watch for powerboats. Carry dam on the right side.

Spider lily along the Lumber River

(11) Nash County Rt. 1746 (below dam) to Sunset Park, downstream from US 64 bridge at Rocky Mount

Drop: 16′	**Time:** 3 hrs.
Difficulty: 1	**Scenery:** A-B
Distance: 7.2 mi.	**Water Quality:** Fair

Gauge: Runnable year round.

Difficulties: Davenport Mill Dam, about eight feet high, is located a little over one mile downstream. It should be approached very cautiously at higher water levels and can be carried on either side--steep on right, longer on left.

(12) Sunset Park, downstream from US 64 bridge at Rocky Mount, to Edgecombe County Rt. 1250 bridge

Drop: 20′	**Time:** 2.5 hrs.
Difficulty: 1-2	**Scenery:** A-B
Distance: 5 mi.	**Water Quality:** Fair

Gauge: Runnable year round. Falls may be scratchy at lower water levels.

Difficulties: The dam at NC 43 bridge should be approached cautiously. At lower levels a carry can be made down a sloping rock on the right side. At higher levels pull out on the left under NC 43 bridge and carry down along the trail in Battle Park. The boulder garden below the dam should be scouted before putting back in.

A put-in can be made at the launching area at the east end of Battle Park for those who don't wish to carry around the dam.

(13) Edgecombe County Rt. 1250 bridge to Rt. 1252 bridge

Drop: 25′	**Time:** 4 hrs.
Difficulty: B	**Scenery:** A
Distance: 12.4 mi.	**Water Quality:** Fair

Gauge: Runnable year round.

Difficulties: None.

(14) Edgecombe County Rt. 1252 bridge to NC 44 bridge (wildlife access area)

Drop: 12´
Difficulty: B
Distance: 11.5 mi.

Time: 4.5 hrs.
Scenery: A
Water Quality: Fair

Gauge: Runnable year round.

Difficulties: None.

(15) NC 44 bridge (wildlife access area) to US Bus. 64 bridge at Riverfront Park in Tarboro

Drop: 10´
Difficulty: B
Distance: 12.2 mi.

Time: 4 hrs.
Scenery: A-B
Water Quality: Fair

Gauge: Runnable year round.

Difficulties: None.
Fishing Creek enters on the left six miles down.

(16) US Bus. 64 bridge at Riverfront Park in Tarboro to NC 42 bridge

Drop: 6´
Difficulty: B
Distance: 7.4 mi.

Time: 2.5 hrs.
Scenery: A
Water Quality: Fair

Gauge: Runnable year round.

Difficulties: None.

(17) NC 42 bridge to the Commons in Greenville (public access area)

Drop: 10´
Difficulty: B
Distance: 19.8 mi.

Time: 6 hrs.
Scenery: A-B
Water Quality: Fair

Gauge: Runnable year round.

Difficulties: None.
Travel on the river below Greenville is possible for many miles, but it is heavily used by powerboats.

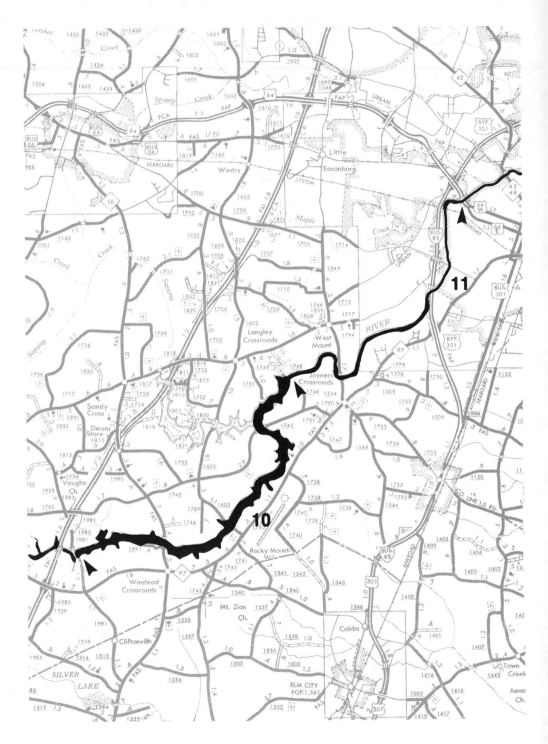

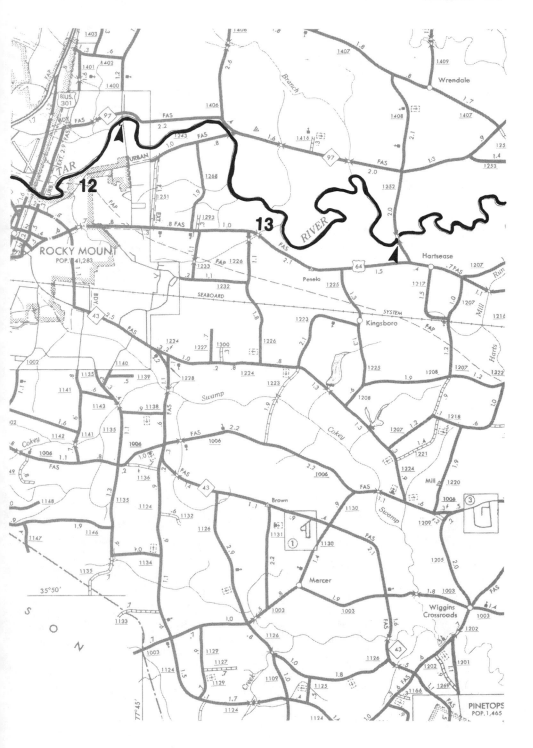

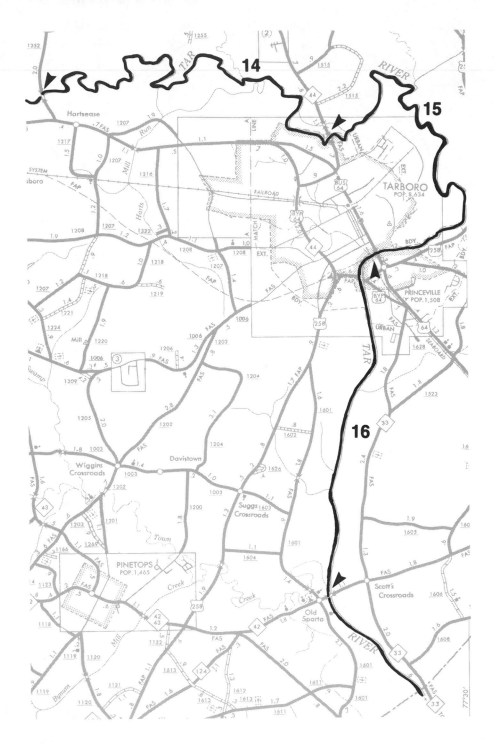

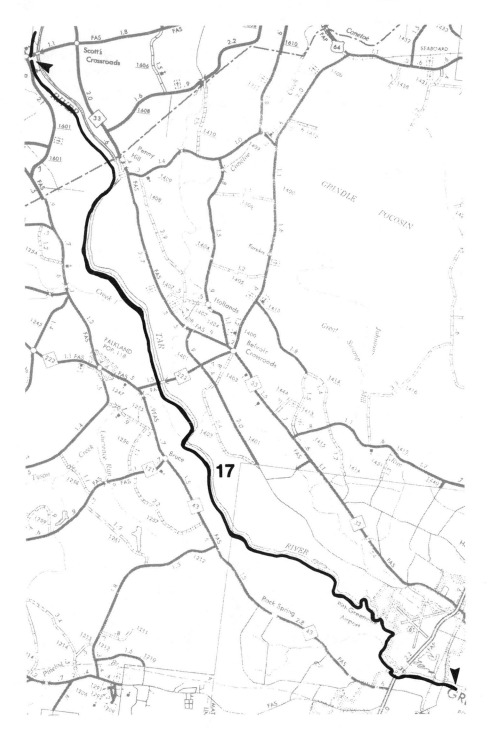

Tranters Creek

Tranters Creek is marginal in that it not only serves as a border between Pitt and Beaufort counties but, depending on rainfall and wind velocity, it may generally be run from west to east or vice versa. For a Coastal Plains stream, its shores are interspersed with relatively high banks. Heron and muskrat may be viewed as well as other animal life inhabiting the cypress, evergreen, and deciduous plants growing along these winding banks.

Topo Maps: Chocowinity, Washington

Counties: Pitt, Beaufort

(1) US 264 bridge to Beaufort County Rt. 1403 bridge

Drop: 0' **Time:** 4.5 hrs.
Difficulty: A **Scenery:** A
Distance: 11 mi. **Water Quality:** Good

Gauge: None. Runnable year round.

Difficulties: None. Access at take-out can sometimes be overgrown.

Directions: *Put-in*--Easternmost bridge of side-by-side bridges on US 264.
Take-out--From put-in, 4.9 miles east to 1403, then south 0.75 miles to a semipublic landing.

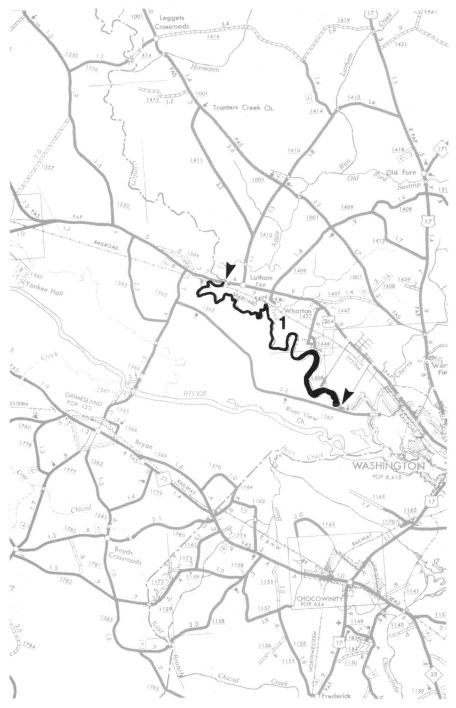

5
Neuse Basin

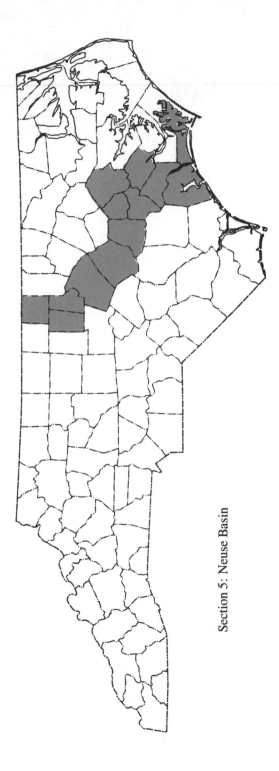

Section 5: Neuse Basin

Brices Creek

Brices Creek heads up in the Croatan National Forest and flows northward through a wilderness setting interrupted only by a North Carolina wildlife access area some five miles down the creek. The area is abundant in animal, bird, and plant life--some of which are unique to the Croatan. The last couple of miles before the take-out are being heavily developed.

Topo Maps: Maysville, New Bern

County: Craven

(1) Craven County Rt. 1111 bridge to Rt. 1004 bridge (access area south of bridge)

Drop: 0′	**Time:** 4.5 hrs.
Difficulty: B	**Scenery:** AA-A-B
Distance: 8 mi.	**Water Quality:** Good

Gauge: None. Runnable year round.

Difficulties: The upper section of this run is rather tight and narrow, and trying to stay out of the bushes may present problems for the inexperienced. This need becomes even more apparent as one becomes aware of the abundance of snakes here. Wind and tide may be a factor at times. During periods of higher water the trip may be extended some four miles by putting in at Rt. 1101 bridge.

Note: Canoes are rented from Merchants Grocery Company which is located at the take-out. They will arrange shuttles for groups.

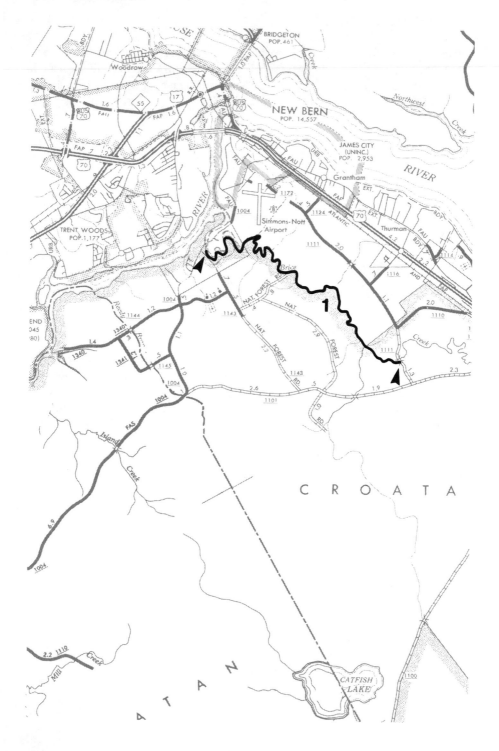

Contentnea Creek

Contentnea Creek* heads up in northern Wilson County and flows southeasterly to join the Neuse River downstream from Kinston. It is primarily a lowland, slow-moving, winding stream flowing through Spanish moss-covered oaks and cypress. The creek meanders among typical coastal floodbanks which quickly become submerged following heavy rains.

Topo Maps: Kinston, Arden

Counties: Greene, Pitt, Lenoir

(1) Wildlife access area at Snow Hill, 1 block east of US 258, to NC 123 bridge at Hookerton

Drop: 9′
Difficulty: A
Distance: 9.5 mi.

Time: 4 hrs.
Scenery: A-B
Water Quality: Good-Fair

Gauge: None. Runnable year round except during very dry spells.

Difficulties: None. Possible carries at lower water levels.

(2) NC 123 bridge at Hookerton to Greene County Rt. 1004 bridge

Drop: 7′
Difficulty: A
Distance: 7.5 mi.

Time: 3-4 hrs.
Scenery: A-B
Water Quality: Good

Gauge: None. See section 1.

Difficulties: The tornadoes of spring 1984 crossed this section and laid a fair amount of debris in the water. Unless it is cleared, passage at low water will prove quite difficult. A bow saw might be handy to take along.

(3) Greene County Rt. 1004 bridge to wildlife access area east of NC 11 on NC 118 and south of the town park in Grifton

Drop: 6′
Difficulty: A
Distance: 8 mi.

Time: 3 hrs.
Scenery: A
Water Quality: Good

---

*From the notes of Ralph Steele and Buster Thompson

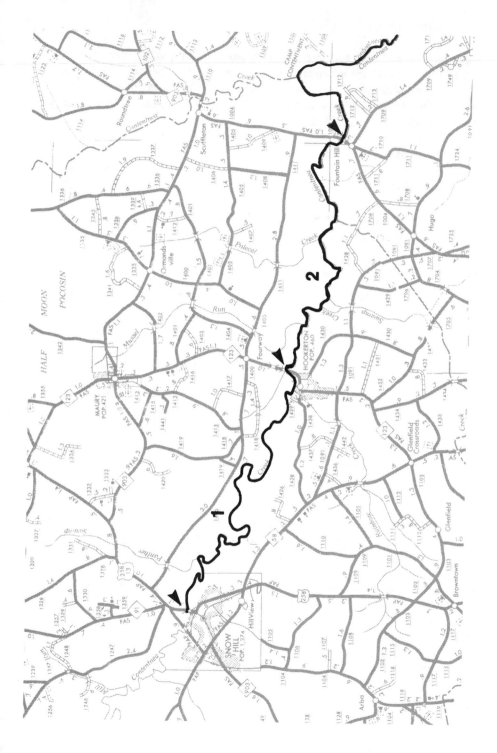

Gauge: None. See section 1.

Difficulties: None, except possible downed trees.

(4) Wildlife access area east of NC 11 on NC 118 and south of the town park in Grifton to Craven County Rt. 1470 bridge over the Neuse River

Drop: 6′

Difficulty: A-B

Distance: 13 mi.

Time: 4.5-5 hrs.

Scenery: A

Water Quality: Good

Gauge: None. See section 1.

Difficulties: About a third of the way down the creek passage is somewhat difficult to locate for a mile or so. This begins at a point opposite what appears to be a dredged area on river left leading directly toward the high TV antennae.

The Neuse is reached seven and a half miles down the creek, with the remaining five and a half miles run on the river.

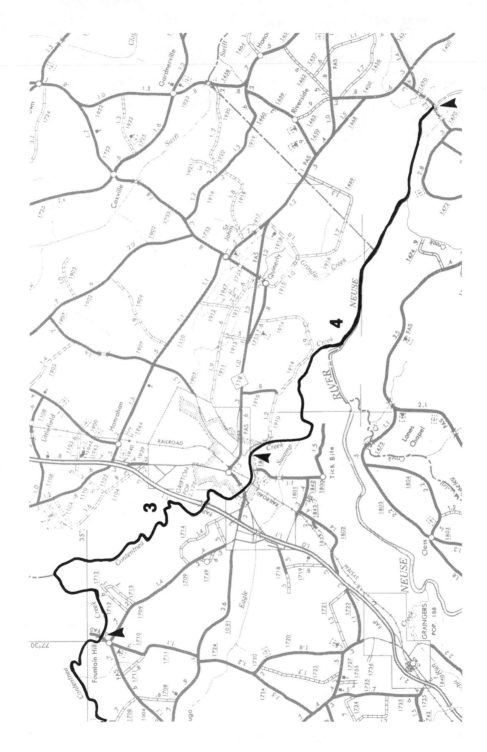

Eno River

The Eno River rises in northwestern Orange County between Carr and McDade. The East Fork is dammed near Cedar Grove to form Lake Orange, then joins the West Fork near Fairfield Church where it is again impounded, this time by Hillsborough as a water supply. This area, called Occoneechee Mountain, has several mines and quarries. Rock used to construct Duke University buildings came from here. The Eno then flows through Duke Forest, used for teaching by the Forestry School, and thereafter traverses a semiwilderness area, surprisingly, since it is located so close to Durham. Many years ago the Eno ran red and blue with wastes from the many small textile plants along its banks. These have long been gone, and nature has so completely reclaimed the river valley that this area has been proposed as a linear park. The State of North Carolina now owns two thirds of the land projected for the already established Eno River State Park. The Association for the Preservation of the Eno River Valley, 4015 Cole Mill Road, Durham, NC 27712, has been very active in efforts to establish the park, in addition to its interest in the history of the area. Canoeists can thank the association for its good work.

Topo Maps: Hillsborough, NW Durham and NE Durham

Counties: Orange, Durham

The Upper Sections in Orange County
Though not often paddled, these can provide an interesting ride at high-water levels.
Faucette Mill Road (SR 1336) to dam above US 70W: Mostly lake, and the City of Hillsborough might not appreciate you paddling in their water supply, but it is done, sometimes.
US 70W to Dimmocks Mill Road (SR 1134): Two miles of easy Class 2s. Too shallow in dry weather.
Dimmocks Mill Road (SR 1134) to NC 86: These three miles are mostly flat and shallow with scenery on the right considerably better than that on the left.
NC 86 to US 70E: Two more miles of the same. Scenery is OK.
US 70E to Lawrence Road (SR 1561): One and a half miles of nice little rapids and better scenery, but fallen trees and logjams may be a problem.

(1) Orange County Rt. 1561 (Lawrence Road) bridge to Cates' (Cades, Cabes, Fews) Ford at end of Rt. 1569

Drop: 60´
Difficulty: 1-2/3
Distance: 4.2 mi.

Time: 2 hrs.
Scenery: A
Water Quality: Good

Big Swamp

Gauge: Orange County Rt. 1567 bridge, Pleasant Green Road. Several gauges have been used in the past. The 3′ staff should be 1′ minimum for solo paddling. Can be run only during wet weather. See also section 6.

Difficulties: After the first mile several small islands appear. Usually run to the left of the first and to the right of the second since the other channels are often tree clogged. The ruins of dams for Berry's Public Mill and Holden's Mill will both be runnable if water is up a bit. Just past the second power line is "Frank's Ledge." Scout! Best run left of center. "Rock Jumble," 100 yards below, is impossible at lower water levels. Just above the take-out is a borderline Class 3, Cates' Ford Ledge; run left over the three-foot break.

Put-in is through private property into a small feeder stream just above the bridge. Ask permission to cross if people are present, and in any case leave the area clean.

(2) Cates' (Cades, Cabes, Fews) Ford at end of Orange County Rt. 1569 to Duke Power Dam at Rt. 1567, Pleasant Green Road

Drop: 15′
Difficulty: 1
Distance: 3 mi.

Time: 1.5 hrs.
Scenery: A
Water Quality: Good

Gauge: See section 1. Pool above dam can be paddled all year.

Difficulties: None. This is an easy beginner's stretch that may be paddled upstream some distance from the old dam. It is also a good place to watch wildlife.

(3) Duke Power Dam at Orange County Rt. 1567, Pleasant Green Road, to Durham County Rt. 1401, Cole Mill Road

Drop: 30′
Difficulty: 1-2/3
Distance: 3.2 mi.

Time: 1.5 hrs.
Scenery: A
Water Quality: Good

Gauge: See section 1.

Difficulties: A little over one mile into the trip is a constricted spot sometimes blocked by fallen trees. A quarter mile farther is an island generally run to the right, but beware of a rock at the bottom of this channel. Very near here was the Cade Mill; remains of two other mills are also nearby, one located along this section. A half mile farther is a long rapid with a strong eddy at the bottom, called Drowning Horse Pool. Legend has it that a drunken miller drove

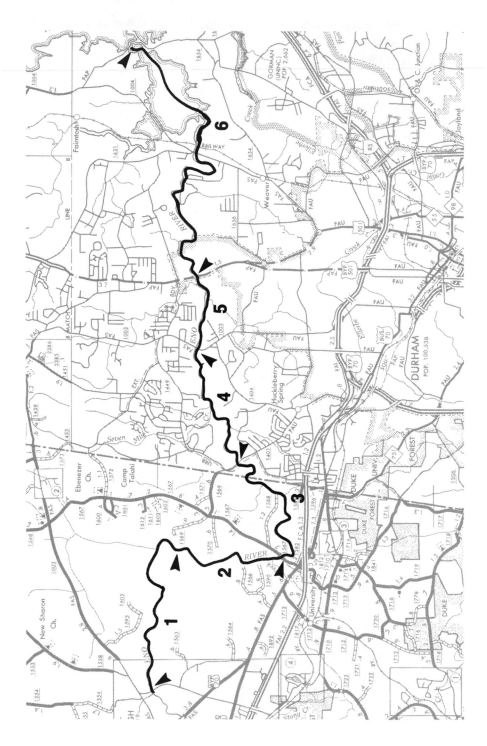

his team and wagon off the cliff and into the river here, killing the horses. The next rapid, Bobbitt's Hole, is narrow and rocky and can become Class 3 at high water. Scout for the narrow, slanting tongue of water on the left.

(4) Durham County Rt. 1401, Cole Mill Road, to Rt. 1003, Guess Road

Drop: 80′
Difficulty: 1-2/3
Distance: 3.2 mi.

Time: 1.5 hrs.
Scenery: A
Water Quality: Good

Gauge: See section 1.

Difficulties: About a mile and a half into the trip is a washed-out dam, and shortly thereafter another, both of which are only short rock garden drops now. The second was the site of the old Durham water supply pumping station, located at Nancy Rhodes Creek. A concrete mill dam, near the end of this section, becomes Class 3 at water levels of three feet. It can be run through the break on the right or down a narrow tongue near the left.

(5) Durham County Rt. 1003, Guess Road, to US 501, Roxboro Road

Drop: 30′
Difficulty: 1-2/3
Distance: 1.7 mi.

Time: 1 hr.
Scenery: A
Water Quality: Good

Gauge: See section 1.

Difficulties: This is a compact but challenging section that can be viewed from the trails along both banks. The first difficulty is the rapid above Sennett's Hole, which has a rock in the left channel and requires a lot of water to open a center channel. Folklore has it that Old Man Sennett came up from Florida in the late 1700s with a box of gold. He built a mill on the river, buried his treasure, and died without revealing its location. Several other rapids are challenging and generally can be run to the left.

Recently a small dam was constructed to supply water power to the reconstructed West Point Mill, the take-out for this trip. When you reach slack water behind this dam, get to the right and portage to the parking lot or else around the dam and the low-water bridge just below. This is a dangerous spot at high-water levels.

Sections 3, 4, and 5 are often done in a single day.

(6) US 501, Roxboro Road, to Durham County Rt. 1632

Drop: 15'   **Time:** 2.5 hrs.
Difficulty: 1   **Scenery:** B
Distance: 7 mi.   **Water Quality:** Fair

Gauge: There is a USGS gauging station located 100 yards downstream from Roxboro Road that is reached from the parking area of the apartments by turning onto Rippling Stream Road near the Exxon station. A minimum reading is 3.0' which corresponds to 270 c.f.s. This gauge can be used for the upper sections as well, with 3.2' minimum.

Difficulties: None. This is a flat trip suitable for beginners and nature lovers. The Eno continues for eight miles to confluence with the Flat, the two forming the Neuse. The distance from Roxboro Road to Durham County Rt. 1004, Old Oxford Road, is three and six-tenths miles and is usually shallow and subject to fallen trees. Subdivision development has occurred along the banks. An additional three and a half miles on the backwaters of Falls Lake brings you to Durham County Rt. 1632, the recommended take-out.

Flat River

The Flat River* rises in Person County, the North Fork near Roxboro and the South Fork near Hurdle Mills. They flow southeasterly, merging just before crossing into Durham County and joining the Eno to form the Neuse.

Topo Map: North Durham

Counties: Person, Durham

(1) Person County Rt. 1739 (end) to Durham County Rt. 1471 bridge near Red Mountain

Drop: 40′
Difficulty: 2-3
Distance: 4 mi.

Time: 2 hrs.
Scenery: A
Water Quality: Good

Gauge: On Route 1614 bridge: 4″ below 0 is minimum for solo. This is a wet-weather run.

Difficulties: The put-in is located below a destroyed mill dam on private property. Ask permission to cross. About one and a half miles into the trip is a dangerous breached dam, a Class 3 drop that can sometimes be run. The second Class 3, within sight of the take-out bridge, is what remains of a stone dam that was breached by high water in 1975. It has a nasty hydraulic across its base.

To find the put-in, go through Rougemont and turn onto Durham County Rt. 1600, which becomes 1739 when it crosses the Person County line.

(2) Durham County Rt. 1471 bridge near Red Mountain to Rt. 1614 bridge

Drop: 5′
Difficulty: 1
Distance: 2 mi.

Time: 1 hr.
Scenery: A
Water Quality: Good

Gauge: On Rt. 1614 bridge; 0 is minimum for solo.

Difficulties: None. A very pleasant, scenic interlude of mostly flatwater through the Hill Forest, which is a teaching and research outpost of the North Carolina State University School of Forestry.

---

*From the notes of Tom McCloud and Allen Trelease.

(3) Durham County Rt. 1614 bridge to Lake Michie at Rt. 1616

Drop: 65′	**Time:** 2 hrs.
Difficulty: 1-2-3	**Scenery:** A
Distance: 4 mi.	**Water Quality:** Good

Gauge: On Rt. 1614 bridge. See section 1.

Difficulties: This is a beautiful little gorge section. After the first quarter mile the gradient increases quickly. A huge, low flattopped rock in the middle of the river lies at the head of an island which is best run to the left since the right is usually tree choked. Three-plus miles down, a low dam develops big souse holes and hydraulics at high-water levels. Portage left after scouting.

The last mile is on the flatwater of Lake Michie with the take-out at the picnic area on the left. There have been occasions in the past when Durham city employees have tried to charge canoeists a fee for the use of their lake. Do not paddle to the far end of the lake and attempt to portage around the dam, which is 80 feet tall. There is no good way around, and city employees have been very unpleasant to people near the dam.

For a map of the Flat River, see page 204.

Little River

This Little River rises in north-central Orange County, less than five miles from the Eno River. Both North and South forks have been paddled at very high water, but barbwire fences and a surprise nine-foot dam (on the South Fork) make it hardly worth the effort. The forks converge east of Guess Road (Rt. 1003) in Durham County, just into section 1.

Topo Map: North Durham

County: Durham

(1) Durham County Rt. 1461 (Johnson Mill Road) bridge to Rt. 1461 bridge (loop)

Drop: 40′   **Time:** 1.5 hrs.
Difficulty: 1-2   **Scenery:** A
Distance: 2.7 mi.   **Water Quality:** Good

Gauge: Gauging station on right bank above US 501 bridge; 1.8′ is minimum for solo because loop road 1461 crosses North and South forks and take-out.

Difficulties: Put-in located on the South Fork. The last half mile is a long rock garden that requires much maneuvering. When you see the bridge, get to shore quickly to avoid being swept downriver.

(2) Durham County Rt. 1461 bridge (loop) to US 501 bridge

Drop: 40′   **Time:** 1 hr.
Difficulty: 1-2-3/4   **Scenery:** A
Distance: 1 mi.   **Water Quality:** Good

Gauge: See section 1. At levels over 3′ the gorge becomes Class 4/5 with big holes and hydraulics. Very dangerous!

Difficulties: The first 200 yards, a fast rock garden, requires tight maneuvering and leads to the first major rapid, which lies at the base of the cliff on river left. This is Swimming Hole Rapid, Class 3, demanding a very tight left-to-right turn. Within another 100 yards, a second cliff marks Fossil Rapid, named because of fossil finds nearby, a Class 3 that becomes a Class 5 with a keeper hydraulic at high-water levels. Another Class 2+ rapid appears after several hundred yards of rock gardens and is marked by a cliff on river right.

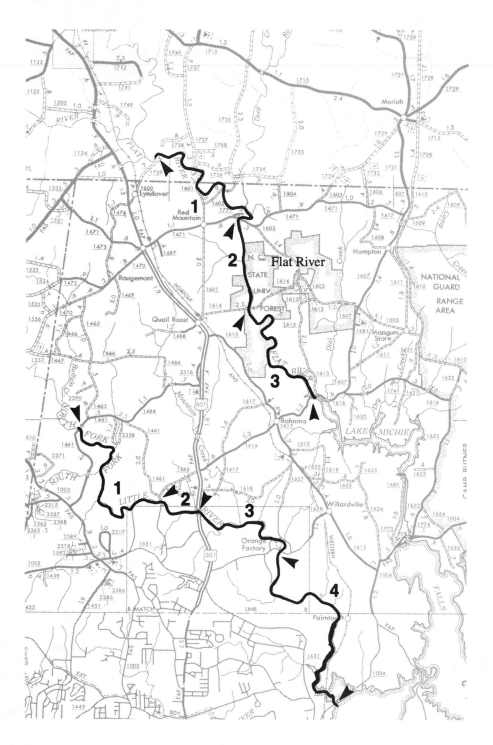

Next, look for a spot where the river splits and take the left channel which funnels down a narrow chute and ends in a Class 3 rapid. Farther on, take the right side of a small island and beware of the Class 2 at its base. It is tricky.

(3) US 501 bridge to Durham County Rt. 1627 at Orange Factory

Drop: 20′
Difficulty: 1-2
Distance: 2.5 mi.

Time: 1.5 hrs.
Scenery: B
Water Quality: Fair+

Gauge: See section 1.

Difficulties: About 150 yards below the US 501 bridge is an old dam which is runnable. At Orange Factory a 15-foot dam has a mandatory portage on the right.

The City of Durham plans to build a water storage reservoir here and is condemning land around Orange Factory, which itself will be submerged. The dam is not supposed to back up water into section 2.

(4) Durham County Rt. 1627 at Orange Factory to Rt. 1004, Old Oxford Highway

Drop: 35′
Difficulty: 1-2
Distance: 6 mi.

Time: 3 hrs.
Scenery: B
Water Quality: Fair

Gauge: See section 1.

Difficulties: None. The backwaters of Falls Lake are entered just beyond the halfway point.

Neuse River

The Neuse River begins at the confluence of the Eno and Flat rivers in Durham County. The first 20 or so miles include the backwaters of Falls of the Neuse Lake. Because of this we pick up the Neuse below the dam at the Falls community. The river breaks gradually through the fall line here as it continues southeasterly across four counties to reach New Bern and Pamlico Sound.

The river was navigable by barge from Smithfield downstream in the early 1800s. Beyond quaint Smithfield Commons, the river passes the unique Cliffs of the Neuse, the village of Seven Springs where the Confederate ram *Neuse* was built, and on downstream to the gunboat's remains at Kinston. Nearby, John Lawson, author of *History of North Carolina*, was captured and later executed by the Tuscarora Indians for traveling upstream from New Bern. This act resulted in the Tuscarora War which began in 1711. It is believed that the river gained its name from the Neusiok, a tribe belonging to the Tuscarora Nation.

From Kinston down, steamboats cruised the river until the 1890s. Later, the clearing of woodlands for agriculture resulted in the river becoming shallow as we find it today.

Topo Maps: Wake Forest, Raleigh East, Garner, Clayton, Selma, Four Oaks, Princeton, Grantham, SW Goldsboro, NW Goldsboro, Williams, Seven Springs, Deep Run NW, Rivermont, Kinston, Ayden, Jasper, Askin, New Bern

Counties: Wake, Johnston, Wayne, Lenoir, Pitt, Craven

(1) Wake County Rt. 2000 bridge to US 401 bridge

Drop: 11′   **Time:** 3 hrs.
Difficulty: 1-2   **Scenery:** B
Distance: 7.7 mi.   **Water Quality:** Good

Gauge: None. Runnable except during extended dry spells.

Difficulties: A small rock garden that runs 150 yards below the put-in. Eight feet of the total 11-foot drop occurs here. This is the proposed site for the Falls Whitewater Training Course.

(2) US 401 bridge to US 64 bridge

Drop: 10′   **Time:** 3.5 hrs.
Difficulty: 1   **Scenery:** A-B
Distance: 7.5 mi.   **Water Quality:** Fair

Gauge: None. Runnable except during long dry periods.

Difficulties: Milburnie Dam, approximately ten feet high, is located a half mile above the take-out. This is an overflow dam that should be approached with caution--especially at high-water levels. It has an extremely long wing on the left, so pull out on the right well above the dam. A carry of some 200 yards is required. Much three-leaf vegetation (poison ivy) is there to keep you company.

(3) US 64 bridge to Wake County Rt. 2555 bridge

Drop: 11′
Difficulty: 1-2
Distance: 6.5 mi.

Time: 2.5 hrs.
Scenery: A-B
Water Quality: Good-Fair

Gauge: None. Runnable year round.

Difficulties: A boulder field three quarters of a mile below the railroad bridge should be scouted at medium to high levels. Generally the safest run will be on the right. About a half mile below the second bridge a ledge forms a fairly good hydraulic at higher water levels.

(4) Wake County Rt. 2555 bridge to NC 42 bridge

Drop: 20′
Difficulty: B-C
Distance: 11 mi.

Time: 4.5 hrs.
Scenery: A
Water Quality: Fair

Gauge: USGS gauge at NC 42 bridge. Runnable year round.

Difficulties: None, except possible downed trees.

(5) NC 42 bridge to Smithfield Commons launching site

Drop: 13′
Difficulty: B
Distance: 12.3 mi.

Time: 5 hrs.
Scenery: A-C
Water Quality: Fair

Gauge: USGS gauge at NC 42 bridge. Runnable year round.

Difficulties: None, except possible downed trees. Commons is located on Front Street, north of US 70 bridge.

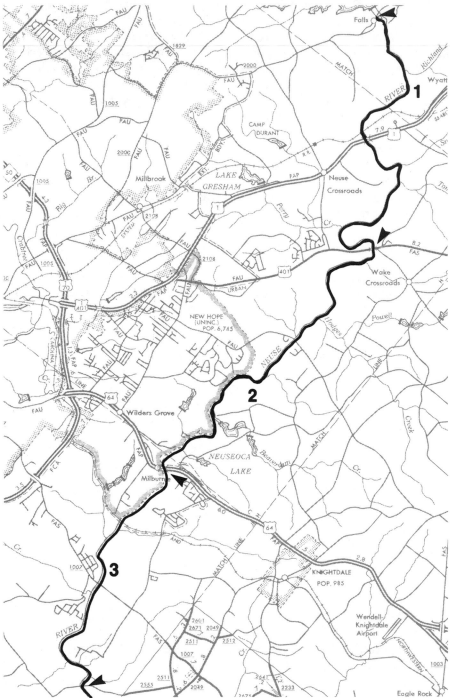

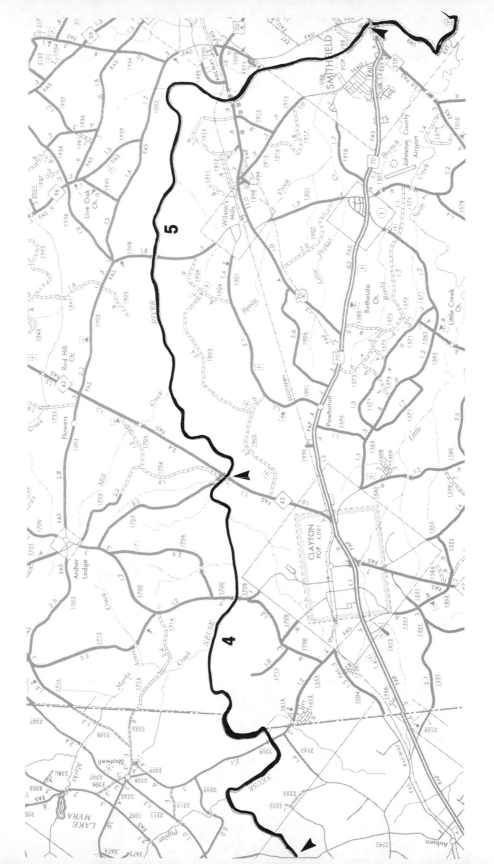

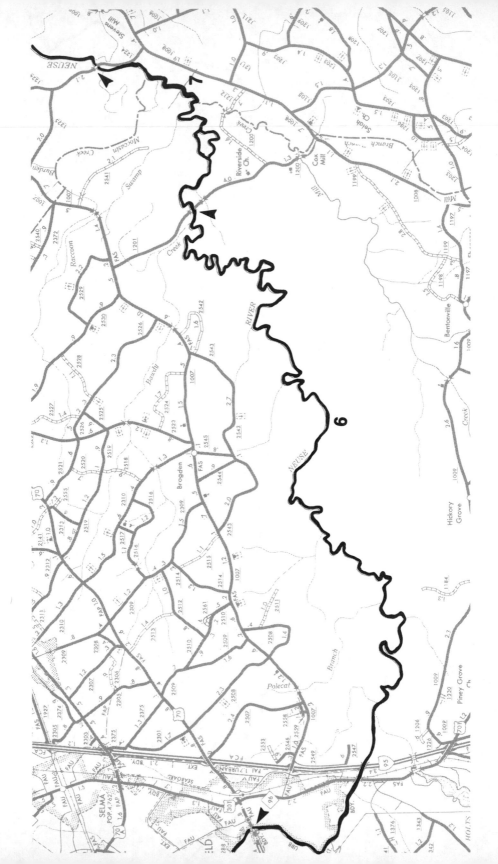

(6) Smithfield Commons launching site to wildlife access area at Johnston County Rt. 1201 bridge

Drop: 28′   **Time:** 12 hrs.
Difficulty: B   **Scenery:** A-C
Distance: 32.5 mi.   **Water Quality:** Good

Gauge: USGS gauge at NC 42 bridge. Runnable year round.

Difficulties: None, except possible downed trees and the inaccessibility after passing beyond NC 96 just three and a half miles below the put-in. The remainder of the section runs through fairly remote country. A good area for wildlife observation.

(7) Wildlife access area at Johnston County Rt. 1201 bridge to wildlife access area at Wayne County Rt. 1224 bridge

Drop: 9′   **Time:** 3 hrs.
Difficulty: B   **Scenery:** A
Distance: 7 mi.   **Water Quality:** Good

Gauge: None. Runnable year round.

Difficulties: None, except downed trees.

(8) Wildlife access area at Wayne County Rt. 1224 bridge to Rt. 1008 bridge

Drop: 10′   **Time:** 3.75 hrs.
Difficulty: B   **Scenery:** B-C
Distance: 9 mi.   **Water Quality:** Good

Gauge: None. Runnable year round.

Difficulties: The ever-present possibility of downed trees and a low head dam that can be extremely dangerous. After passing the Carolina Power and Light power plant, the river makes a big bend north. CP&L has cut a channel across this bend that should not be attempted; continue around the bend. As soon as markers in the river above the dam are sighted, begin moving left and take out in the power line cut for a 75-yard carry to a point well below the dam. A long reversal current below the dam can carry the unwary back into the hydraulic. Several drownings have occurred here, so *beware!*

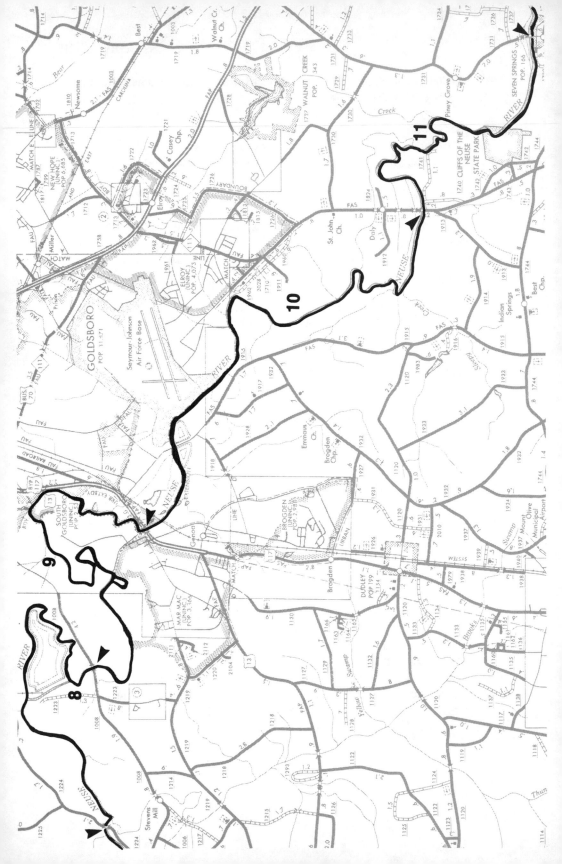

(9) Wayne County Rt. 1008 bridge to wildlife access area at US 117 bridge

Drop: 10′
Difficulty: B
Distance: 9.8 mi.

Time: 4 hrs.
Scenery: B-C
Water Quality: Good-Fair

Gauge: None. Runnable year round.

Difficulties: Again the river makes a large bend to the north. A man-made channel with a low dam has been cut across this bend. Under normal water levels this channel cannot be run. Stay with the main riverbed at higher levels to be safe.

(10) Wildlife access area at US 117 bridge to NC 111 bridge

Drop: 11′
Difficulty: B
Distance: 12.7 mi.

Time: 5 hrs.
Scenery: B
Water Quality: Good

Gauge: None. Runnable year round.

Difficulties: None, except the possibility of downed trees.

(11) NC 111 bridge to Wayne County Rt. 1731 bridge at Seven Springs

Drop: 5′
Difficulty: B
Distance: 8 mi.

Time: 3.25 hrs.
Scenery: A
Water Quality: Good

Gauge: None. Can be run all year.

Difficulties: None.
Some six miles down this section the banks on the right will begin to rise slowly into high bluffs, which indicates your entry into the Cliffs of the Neuse State Park, a nice place to visit and break your trip.

(12) Wayne County Rt. 1731 bridge at Seven Springs to Lenoir County 1152 bridge

Drop: 4′
Difficulty: B
Distance: 6 mi.

Time: 2.5 hrs.
Scenery: A
Water Quality: Good

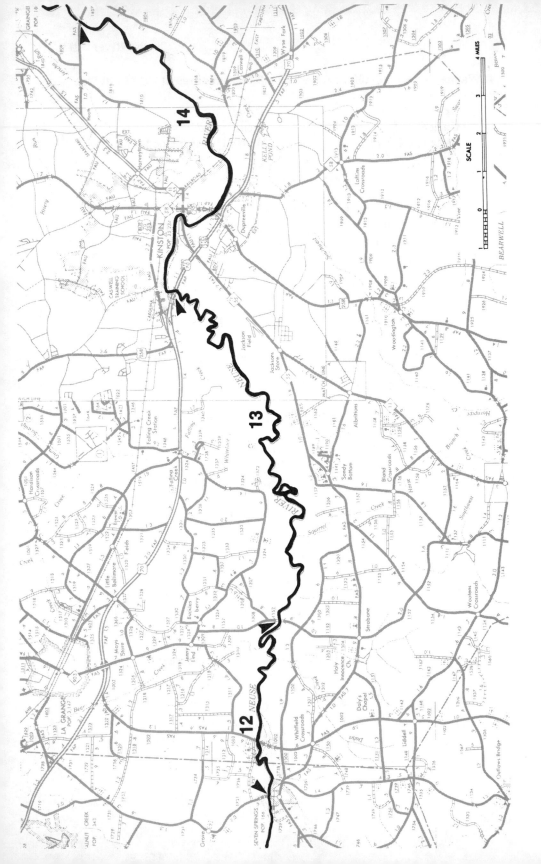

Gauge: None. Can be run all year.

Difficulties: None.

(13) Lenoir County 1152 bridge to wildlife access area at US 70W

Drop: 11 ′   **Time:** 5.25 hrs.
Difficulty: B   **Scenery:** A-B
Distance: 12.8 mi.   **Water Quality:** Good

Gauge: None. Can be run year round.

Difficulties: None.

(14) Wildlife access area at US 70W to NC 55 bridge

Drop: 9 ′   **Time:** 4.5 hrs.
Difficulty: B   **Scenery:** A-C
Distance: 11.5 mi.   **Water Quality:** Good

Gauge: None. Can be run year round.

Difficulties: None.

A short distance downstream on the left lie the remains of the Confederate gunboat *Neuse*, which engaged the Union forces advancing on Kinston before being scuttled by her commander in order to prevent her capture. This occurred some five miles downriver. After many problems the 500-ton hull was raised and moved to this site in 1964. It is a short walk to the Neuse and the visitor center.

(15) NC 55 bridge to Craven County Rt. 1470 bridge

Drop: 8 ′   **Time:** 6.5 hrs.
Difficulty: B   **Scenery:** A
Distance: 15 mi.   **Water Quality:** Good

Gauge: None. Can be run all year.

Difficulties: None.

An earlier take-out can be made at Cowpen Landing at the foot of Rt. 1441, cutting off three miles.

Contentnea Creek enters on the left about nine miles downriver.

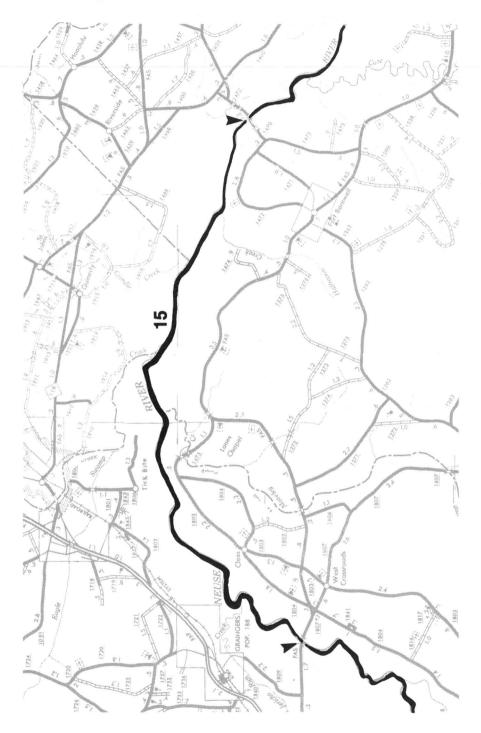

(16) Craven County Rt. 1470 bridge to Rt. 1400 bridge

    Drop: 0′   **Time:** 6.5 hrs.
    Difficulty: A-B   **Scenery:** A
    Distance: 15.5 mi.   **Water Quality:** Good

    Gauge: None. Can be run all year.

    Difficulties: The river enters tidelands with marshes where the channel must be followed closely. Winds and tides can be factors.

(17) Craven County Rt. 1400 bridge to wildlife access area 1 mile north of Bridgeton off US 17 east of New Bern

    Drop: 0′   **Time:** 4 hrs.
    Difficulty: A-B   **Scenery:** A-C
    Distance: 9 mi.   **Water Quality:** Good

    Gauge: None. Can be run all year.

    Difficulties: See section 16.
    A later take-out can be made by continuing one and a half miles to Bus. 70 bridge.

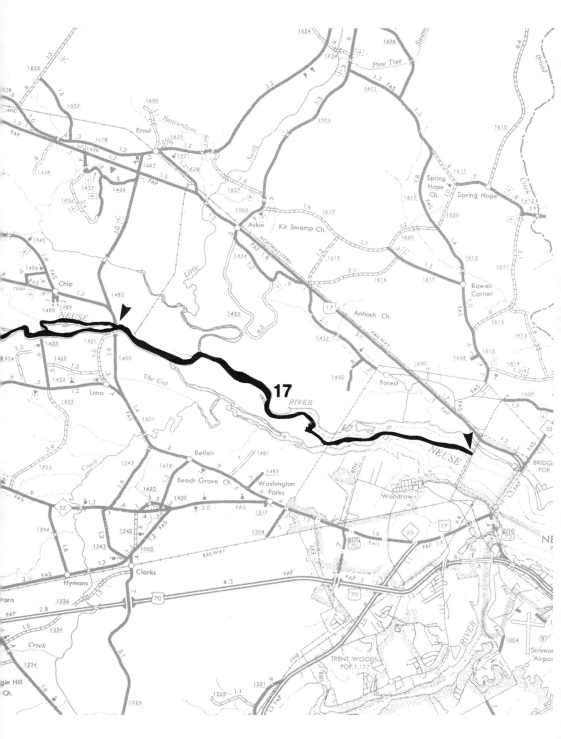

Trent River

The Trent River heads up in Lenoir County and flows southeast across Jones County to Pollocksville, where it bears northeast to join the Neuse at New Bern. This black water stream flows primarily through remote areas with a few exceptions.

French settled about two miles up the river in 1707. Royal Governor William Tryon toured much of what was then North Carolina before selecting the banks of the Trent as the seat for his provincial government and building Tryon Palace in 1767-1770. The river was used by steamers as far as Trenton on a regular basis for a number of years.

The river is cleared periodically of snags by the county for mosquito control.

Topo Maps: Trent River, New Bern

Counties: Jones, Craven

(1) Jones County Rt. 1129 bridge to NC 58 bridge

Drop: 0′   **Time:** 2.5 hrs.
Difficulty: B   **Scenery:** A-B
Distance: 5.2 mi.   **Water Quality:** Good

Gauge: None. Runnable only during wet seasons.

Difficulties: Downed trees of which there can be many.

(2) NC 58 bridge to Jones County Rt. 1300 bridge

Drop: 0′   **Time:** 3 hrs.
Difficulty: B   **Scenery:** A-B
Distance: 6.8 mi.   **Water Quality:** Good

Gauge: None. Runnable only during wet seasons.

Difficulties: Downed trees of which there can be many.

(3) Jones County Rt. 1300 bridge to Rt. 1001 bridge at Trenton

Drop: 0′   **Time:** 4.5 hrs.
Difficulty: B   **Scenery:** A-B
Distance: 10.4 mi.   **Water Quality:** Good

Gauge: None. Runnable except during drier seasons.

Difficulties: Some downed trees.

(4) Jones County Rt. 1001 bridge at Trenton to Rt. 1121 bridge

Drop: 0′	**Time:** 5 hrs.
Difficulty: B	**Scenery:** A
Distance: 14 mi.	**Water Quality:** Good

Gauge: None. Can be run most of the year.

Difficulties: Possibly some downed trees.

(5) Jones County Rt. 1121 bridge to public ramp 50 yards below US 17 bridge in Pollocksville

Drop: 0′	**Time:** 3 hrs.
Difficulty: B	**Scenery:** A
Distance: 9 mi.	**Water Quality:** Good

Gauge: None. Runnable year round.

Difficulties: None.

(6) US 17 bridge (public ramp 50 yards below) in Pollocksville to Craven County Rt. 1004 bridge over Brice Creek (1 mile up creek, which is first open waterway on right after heavy residential development begins)

Drop: 0′	**Time:** 6.5 hrs.
Difficulty: A-B	**Scenery:** A-B
Distance: 15.5 mi.	**Water Quality:** Good

Gauge: None. Runnable year round.

Difficulties: None, except tides and winds in lower section.
An easy take-out can be made at the mouth of the Neuse at US 70 bridge by continuing two miles beyond the mouth of Brice Creek.

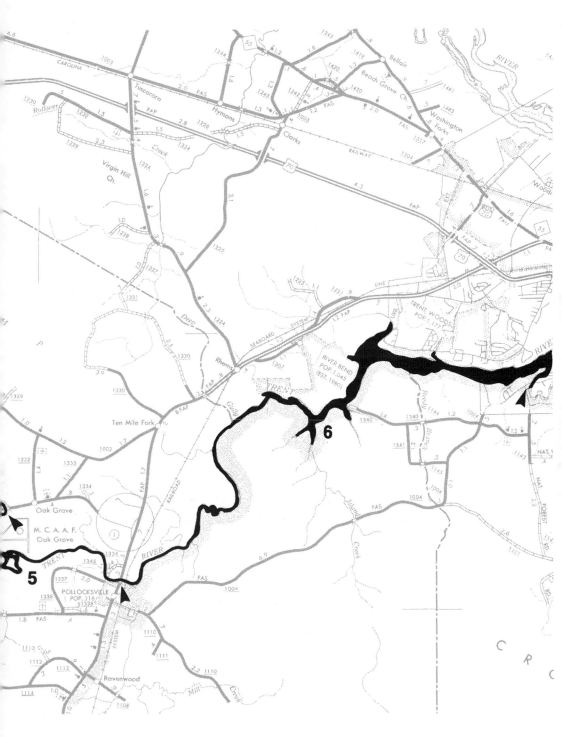

White Oak River

The White Oak River heads up in the center of White Oak Pocasin in northern Onslow County and flows generally southeast some 50 miles before emptying into the Atlantic at Bogue Inlet. The river that borders on the western edge of the Croatan National Forest holds an abundance of wildlife, especially in the Black Swamp below Maysville.

Topo Maps: Jacksonville N.E., Maysville

Counties: Jones, Onslow, Carteret

(1) US 17 bridge at Belgrade to wildlife access area (Haywood's Landing) off NC 58, 7.5 miles southeast of Maysville.

Drop: 0′	**Time:** 3.5 hrs.
Difficulty: B-A-1	**Scenery:** A
Distance: 8.8 mi.	**Water Quality:** Good

Gauge: None. Runnable year round.

Difficulties: Two low ledges downstream from the put-in present a pleasant surprise from what is expected in this flat country. A short distance downstream from the second ledge, the first of a series of lakes is entered. Bear right as you enter, take the right channel through the second, bear left across the third, head straight across the fourth to a small outlet, then bear left and proceed down the length of the fifth and last lake.

Farther downstream, the river breaks into two or three channels a number of times. Observe the current closely and follow it.

(2) Wildlife access area (Haywood's Landing) off NC 58, 7.5 miles southeast of Maysville, to Carteret County Rt. 1101 and Onslow County Rt. 1442 bridge.

Drop: 0′	**Time:** 3-4 hrs.
Difficulty: B-A	**Scenery:** AA-A
Distance: 7.5 mi.	**Water Quality:** Good

Gauge: None. Runnable year round.

Difficulties: None, except possible head winds that may be encountered in the salt marshes.

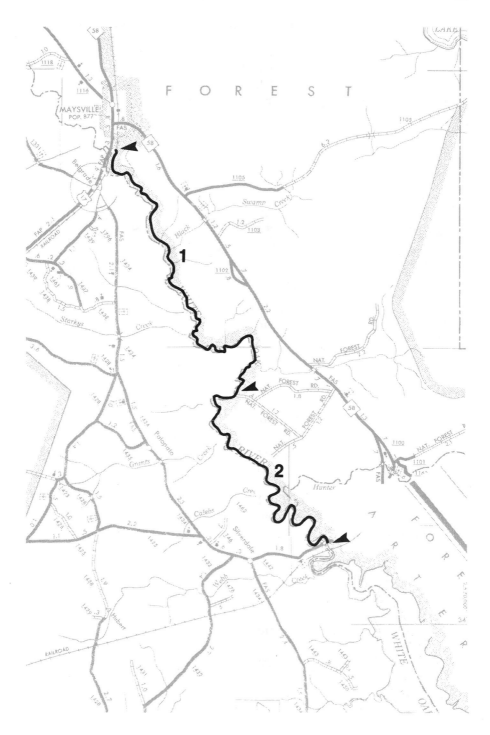

Directions: *Take-out*--On the east bank just below the bridge at a private access area ($1 fee), or some 200 yards west of the bridge at a small flat area on the south side of the river.

Lockwood Folly River

6

Lumber Basin

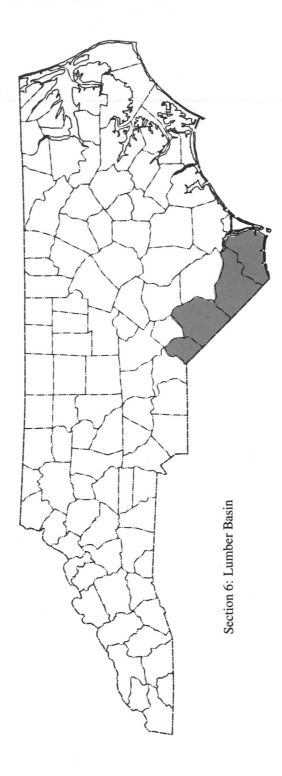

Section 6: Lumber Basin

Big Swamp

Big Swamp heads up in northern Robeson County and winds its way south just inside the county on the east side until it confluences with the Lumber River upstream from Boardman.

This is a true swamp that can be reasonably negotiated at times of high water. At lower levels the story is quite different. One can make a short trip upstream for a mile or so into a most scenic area at low levels.

Topo Map: Chadbourn

Counties: Robeson, Columbus

(1) Wildlife access area at Robeson County Rt. 1002 bridge (Lennon's Bridge) to US 74 bridge (Ivey's Bridge)

Drop: 3′   **Time:** 2.5-4 hrs.
Difficulty: A-B   **Scenery:** A
Distance: 6.2 mi.   **Water Quality:** Good

Gauge: None. Runnable only during periods of higher water.

Difficulties: Primarily downed trees and some problems in locating the main channel at medium water levels. At lower levels there will be tree after tree to pull over. Don't be lured into a trip after looking at the nice open area at Lennon's Bridge. Downstream the passage closes in quickly.

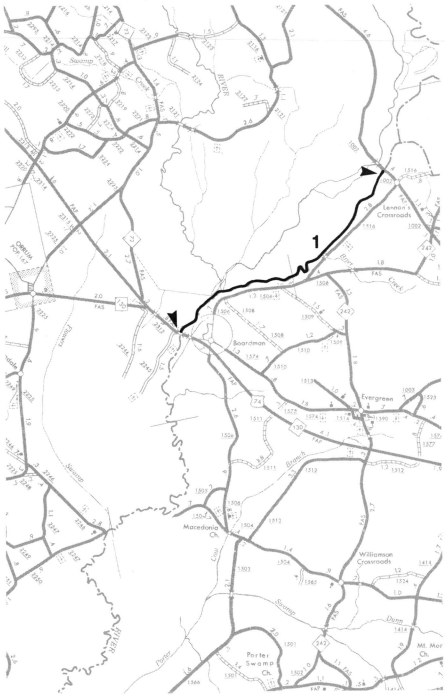

Lockwood Folly River

Lockwood Folly is a black water river that begins in a coastal swamp filled with bird life. Hawks, herons, pileated woodpeckers, and ospreys are abundant here. There are other critters as well, so don't neglect the water level while searching for wildlife. Once, while paddling slowly along, searching for signs of life in one of the many osprey nests, one of the authors and his wife had their wits, as well as their canoe, rattled by a sudden bellow from a 9-foot gator not 15 feet away. Their new-found friend then proceeded to swim alongside for some distance as if escorting them on their way.

About halfway through the run, the river breaks out of the swamp and enters the marshes where it meanders back and forth until it reaches Varnum.

Topo Maps: Supply, Holden Beach

County: Brunswick

(1) NC 211 bridge south of Supply to Varnum at end of Brunswick County Rt. 1122

Drop: 0 ′   **Time:** 3-4.5 hrs.
Difficulty: A   **Scenery:** A
Distance: 9 mi.   **Water Quality:** Good

Gauge: None. Runnable year round.

Difficulties: None, except strong winds that may occur in the marshes. Easy take-out at ramp next to Garland's Seafood Market.

For those who don't have a shuttle, a round trip can be made by timing your run to Varnum with the outgoing tide and the return trip with the incoming tide.

If one feels inclined to explore upstream from NC 211, do just that! But don't be misled by the seemingly clear section of water seen from the next bridge upstream, Rt. 1501. Within 100 yards it becomes all but impassable on the water. Do your paddling "up" from NC 211.

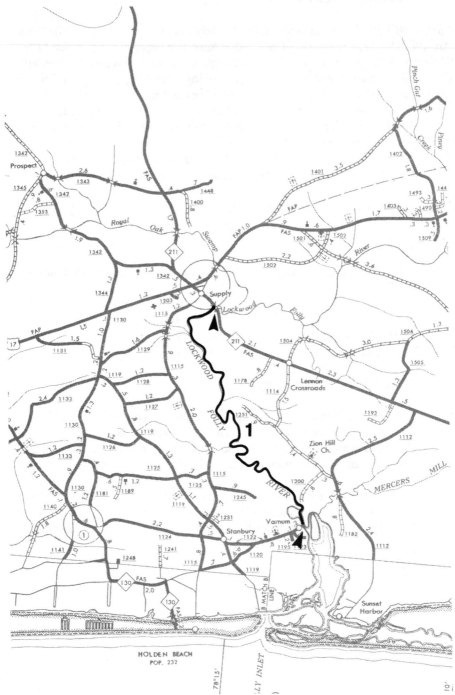

Lumber River and Drowning Creek

The Lumber River rises as Drowning Creek in the sandhills of Moore County. After entering Scotland County Drowning Creek is joined by Buffalo Creek, and the Lumber is born. It then flows south along the east side of Scotland County and east across Robeson County before turning south again and entering South Carolina. It falls into the Little Pee Dee a few miles below Nichols, South Carolina.

Early settlers called it Drowning Creek because of its "whirlpools." The Indians called it the Lumbee, which was later changed to Lumber because of the amount of timber rafted downstream to Georgetown in the early 1800s.

The first settlers wrote of the Lumbee Indians speaking English. This led many to think that they descended from a mixed race that had moved from the Neuse-Pamlico region and had previously assimilated Sir Walter Raleigh's Lost Colony.

The Lumber River flows out of the sandhills through an area known as "the flatwoods" (the Coastal Plain) before entering predominately swampy terrain east and south of Lumberton.

The length of river described within North Carolina has been recognized by the state as a state trail. The section in Scotland County, the Lumber River Canoe Trail, is the first state "canoe trail," while the section from NC 71 to Fair Bluff has been designated the Lower Lumber River Recreation Trail. Establishment of these two stretches was the result of a few people who had the foresight to recognize the value of such an outstanding natural recreational resource. Their efforts hopefully will give future generations an opportunity to enjoy the river. Our thanks go to Bill Scott of Laurinburg and David and Donna Scott of Fair Bluff, who led this movement and allowed us to share in their love for the Lumber River.

Topo Maps: Pine Bluff, Silver Hill, Wagram, Wakulla, Maxton, Pembroke, McDonald, South West Lumberton, North West Lumberton, Bladenboro, Chadbourn, Fair Bluff

Counties: Scotland, Robeson, Columbus

(1) US 15-501 bridge over Drowning Creek to Scotland County Rt. 1412 bridge

Drop: 28′	**Time:** 4.5 hrs.
Difficulty: B	**Scenery:** A
Distance: 9.4 mi.	**Water Quality:** Good

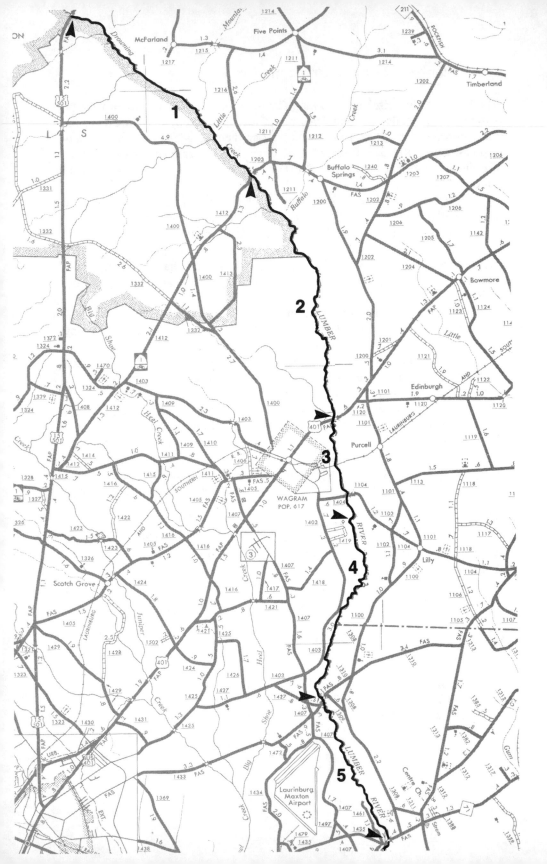

Gauge: None. Runnable year round. Downed trees can become a greater factor at lower water levels when estimating paddling times.

Difficulties: None, except possible downed trees.

(2) Scotland County Rt. 1412 bridge to wildlife access area at US 401 bridge

Drop: 12′
Difficulty: A-B
Distance: 10.5 mi.

Time: 4 hrs.
Scenery: A
Water Quality: Good

Gauge: None. See section 1.

Difficulties: None, except possible downed trees.
Cypress Bend Campsite, accessible only by canoe, is located about seven miles downstream from the put-in. Please haul out what you bring in.

(3) Wildlife access area at US 401 bridge to Riverton Park off Scotland County Rt. 1404 east of Wagram

Drop: 3′
Difficulty: A
Distance: 3 mi.

Time: 1 hr.
Scenery: A-B
Water Quality: Good

Gauge: See section 1.

Difficulties: None, except possible downed trees.

(4) Riverton Park off Scotland County Rt. 1404 east of Wagram to Rt. 1433 (McGirts Bridge)

Drop: 16′
Difficulty: A
Distance: 9.2 mi.

Time: 3 hrs.
Scenery: A-B
Water Quality: Good

Gauge: See section 1.

Difficulties: None, except possible downed trees.

(5) Scotland County Rt. 1433 bridge (McGirts Bridge) to NC 71 bridge north of Maxton

Drop: 16'   **Time:** 3 hrs.
Difficulty: A   **Scenery:** A
Distance: 7.3 mi.   **Water Quality:** Good

Gauge: See section 1.

Difficulties: None, except possible downed trees.

(6) NC 71 bridge north of Maxton to Robeson County Rt. 1153 bridge at Alma

Drop: 8'   **Time:** 2.5 hrs.
Difficulty: A   **Scenery:** A-B
Distance: 5.8 mi.   **Water Quality:** Good

Gauge: See section 1.

Difficulties: None, except possible downed trees.

(7) Robeson County Rt. 1153 bridge at Alma to Rt. 1354 bridge

Drop: 12'   **Time:** 2.5 hrs.
Difficulty: A   **Scenery:** A
Distance: 5.9 mi.   **Water Quality:** Good

Gauge: See section 1.

Difficulties: None, except possible downed trees.

(8) Robeson County Rt. 1354 bridge to Rt. 1554 bridge

Drop: 12'   **Time:** 3.5 hrs.
Difficulty: A   **Scenery:** A
Distance: 7.2 mi.   **Water Quality:** Good

Gauge: See section 1.

Difficulties: None, except possible downed trees.

(9) Robeson County Rt. 1554 bridge to Rt. 1550 bridge

Drop: 15'   Time: 3.5 hrs.
Difficulty: A   Scenery: A
Distance: 8 mi.   Water Quality: Good

Gauge: See section 1.

Difficulties: None, except possible downed trees.

(10) Robeson County Rt. 1550 bridge to wildlife access area at NC 72 bridge

Drop: 16'   Time: 4 hrs.
Difficulty: A   Scenery: A
Distance: 9.5 mi.   Water Quality: Good

Gauge: See section 1.

Difficulties: None, except possible downed trees.

(11) Wildlife access area at NC 72 bridge to NC 41 bridge

Drop: 6'   Time: 2.5 hrs.
Difficulty: A   Scenery: A-B-C
Distance: 5.4 mi.   Water Quality: Good

Gauge: See section 1.

Difficulties: None, except possible downed trees.

(12) NC 41 bridge to wildlife access area at Robeson County Rt. 1620 (Old 74) bridge

Drop: 4'   Time: 1.5 hrs.
Difficulty: A   Scenery: A-B-C
Distance: 3.6 mi.   Water Quality: Good

Gauge: See section 1.

Difficulties: None.

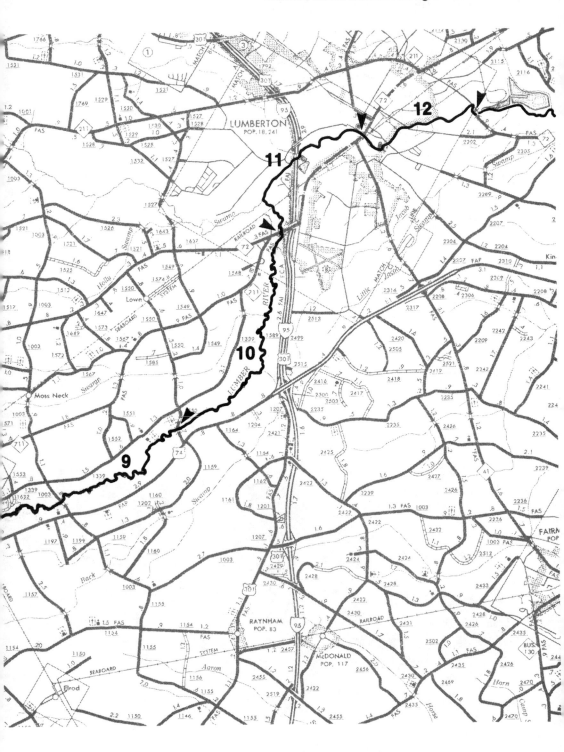

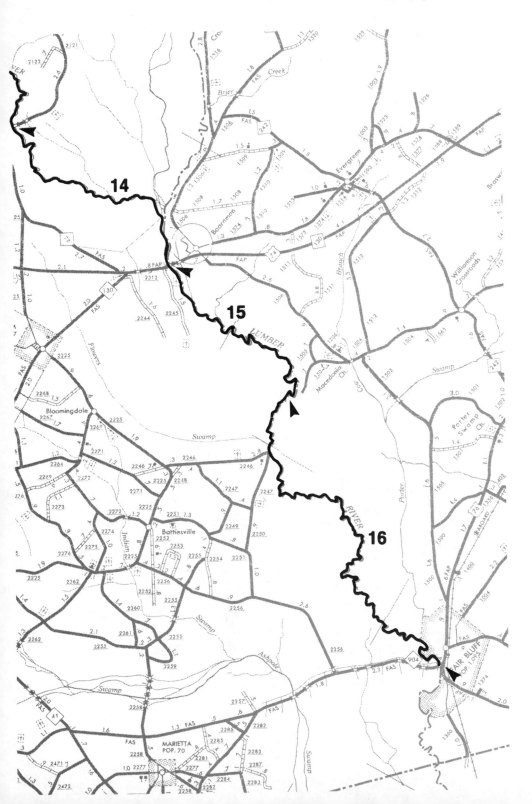

(13) Wildlife access area at Robeson County Rt. 1620 (Old 74) bridge to Rt. 2121 bridge

Drop: 10′
Difficulty: A
Distance: 11.2 mi.

Time: 5.5 hrs.
Scenery: A-B-C
Water Quality: Good

Gauge: See section 1

Difficulties: None, except possible downed trees.

(14) Robeson County Rt. 2121 bridge to US 74 bridge at Boardman

Drop: 12′
Difficulty: A
Distance: 7.6 mi.

Time: 4 hrs.
Scenery: A
Water Quality: Good

Gauge: See section 1.

Difficulties: None.
Big Swamp enters about five and a half miles down on the left.

(15) US 74 bridge at Boardman to red barn (northwest of Macedonia Church) at end of Columbus County Rt. 1504

Drop: 5′
Difficulty: A
Distance: 6.2 mi.

Time: 3 hrs.
Scenery: A
Water Quality: Good

Gauge: See section 1.

Difficulties: This section is generally open, but be on the lookout for possible blowdowns.

(16) Red barn (northwest of Macedonia Church) at end of Columbus County Rt. 1504 to NC 904 bridge at Fair Bluff

Drop: 13′
Difficulty: A
Distance: 15.2 mi.

Time: 6 hrs.
Scenery: A
Water Quality: Good

Gauge: See section 1.

Difficulties: None, except an occasional blowdown, but generally the entire course is open.

(17) NC 904 bridge at Fair Bluff to US 76 bridge at Nichols, South Carolina

Drop: 14′	**Time:** 7 hrs.
Difficulty: A	**Scenery:** A
Distance: 17.2 mi.	**Water Quality:** Good

Gauge: See section 1.

Difficulties: None.

Some five miles down from Nichols the Lumber joins the Little Pee Dee. The next take-out will be SC 917 bridge, approximately seven miles below the confluence.

Cruising the Lumber River at high water

Waccamaw River

The Waccamaw River heads up in Lake Waccamaw and flows south across the intriguing Green Swamp before turning southwest to form the line between Columbus and Brunswick counties. It then enters South Carolina and flows some 70 miles to confluence with the Pee Dee River and form Winyah Bay at Georgetown.

Lake Waccamaw, fed by natural springs, is believed to have been formed by a huge meteorite thousands of years ago. It was first mentioned in 1734 by William Bartram in his "Journal of Travels." Osceola, chief of the Seminoles during the Seminole Wars, is believed to have been born on the lakeshore near Dupree Landing.

The Green Swamp, a wilderness not to be entered by the unprepared, abounds in wildlife. Crusoe Island on the southern edge of the swamp was settled in the 1790s by French citizens who had escaped from the Isle of Haiti during the war between the French and Negro slaves. Their descendants are a uniquely independent people.

Early on, the river was used by rafts and barges up to 30 feet wide hauling logs, turpentine, and shingles as far up as Old Dock. At a later time an old side-wheel steamer made weekly runs as far upstream as Pireway. At "Mule's Ear," a sharp bend in the river between Pireway and the South Carolina line, loggers spent two nights in the same spot because it took them a day to travel around the bend. The river has diminished considerably in size since those days, primarily due to poor logging practices.

Topo Maps: Whiteville, Old Dock, Freeland, Pireway, NC; Longs, NC and SC

Counties: Columbus, Brunswick, NC; Horry, SC

(1) Lake Waccamaw to Columbus County Rt. 1928 bridge east of Old Dock

Drop: 11 ′   **Time:** 6-7 hrs.
Difficulty: A-B   **Scenery:** A
Distance: 11 mi.   **Water Quality:** Good-Fair

Gauge: None. Runnable primarily during periods of higher water.

Difficulties: Downed trees primarily. For those inclined toward shortcuts, the possibility of getting lost definitely exists. Stay with the channel.

For the next several miles the Green Swamp, which abounds with wildlife, will be your home. Four miles below the dam, the river forks. Bear left.

Waccamaw River at high water

Houses on the left about halfway down belong to the inhabitants of Crusoe Island; one may want to stop and visit, as well as look over their dugout canoes. The first high ground lies about nine miles downstream on the left. White Marsh Creek enters at mile ten. Bear to the left at this point.

Directions: *Put-in*--One has three choices for possible entry: (1) Weavers Landing on the north side of the lake, which requires a 1.6 mile paddle to the dam; (2) Dupree Landing on the west side, which is 1.1 miles from the dam; and (3) south on Columbus County Rt. 1735 from US 74-76, then right on NC 214 to Rt. 1967 for some 6 miles to dam. Road conditions can be very poor in wet weather.

(2) Columbus County Rt. 1928 bridge east of Old Dock to NC 130 bridge

Drop: 8′   **Time:** 4-5 hrs.
Difficulty: A-B   **Scenery:** A-B
Distance: 12.9 mi.   **Water Quality:** Fair

Gauge: None. Runnable year round, except during very dry periods.

Difficulties: None, except possible downed trees.
The next high ground is located about three miles downstream; beyond that point there are occasional high grounds throughout the remainder of this section.

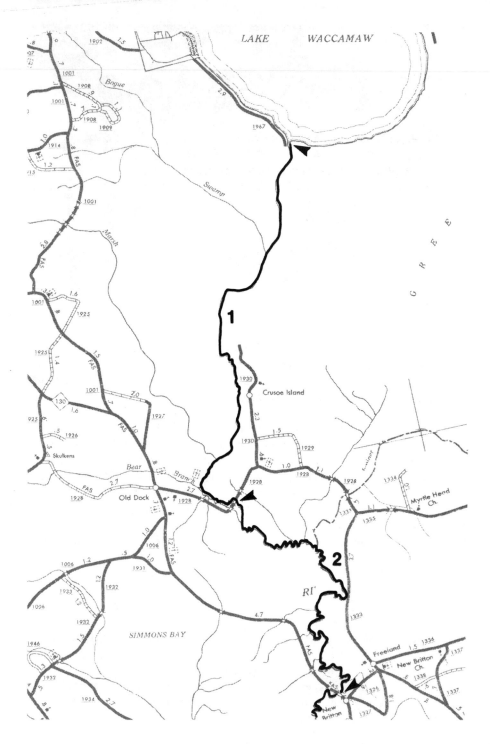

(3) NC 130 bridge to wildlife access area at NC 904 bridge southeast of Pireway

    Drop: 10′   **Time:** 7-8 hrs.
    Difficulty: A-B   **Scenery:** A-B
    Distance: 18.1 mi.   **Water Quality:** Fair

    Gauge: None. Runnable year round.

    Difficulties: None, except possible downed trees.
This area is mostly swamp with few campsites, so one shouldn't pass up too many opportunities to stop if darkness is approaching. The river is much wider and much slower in its lower reaches than in the upper.

(4) Wildlife access area at NC 904 bridge southeast of Pireway to SC 9 bridge

    Drop: 9′   **Time:** 6-7 hrs.
    Difficulty: A-B   **Scenery:** A-B
    Distance: 19.8 mi.   **Water Quality:** Fair

    Gauge: None. Runnable year round.

    Difficulties: None, except downed trees in the swamp.
The river narrows considerably about three and a half miles down from the put-in. Three channels are evident at this point. Go left. Two channels become evident beyond here. Go right. The River Swamp is on the west and the Cawcaw Swamp on the east for the next few miles. At normal water levels one will find many campsites on low bluffs and sandbars above and below the swamps.
A take-out can be made at Horry's Fish House above the bridge. Ask permission before leaving a car here.

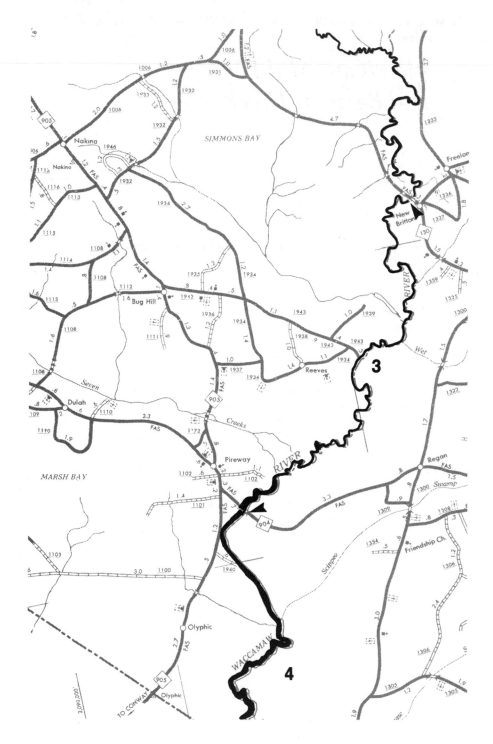

7

Merchants Mill Pond and Bennetts Creek

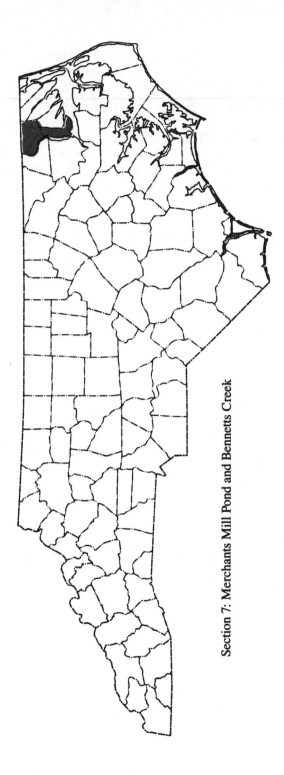

Section 7: Merchants Mill Pond and Bennetts Creek

Merchants Mill Pond and Bennetts Creek

The Chowan Swamp Canoe Trail is located in the far northeastern corner of the state and connects Merchants Mill Pond, seven feet above sea level, with the tidal waters of the Chowan River. The millpond, impounded 170 years ago, and nearly 1,000 acres of Chowan Swamp along Bennetts Creek are a recent addition to the North Carolina Parks System. There is a small campground in the park for use by those who wish a day-trip. The park office may be contacted at Route 1, Box 141-A, Gatesville, NC 27938, phone (919) 357-1911.

The straight-line distance across Merchants Mill Pond is only four and seven-tenths miles, but this is not a trip for those in a hurry. Sit quietly, watch, and listen to the life in the swamp. Birds and reptiles abound. Cypress and swamp tupelos grow in abundance, as well as many other water-tolerant plants. A trail, marked by buoys, leads you up the lake or to an overnight camping area if you wish to camp from your canoe.

Bennetts Creek begins its run through the dense Chowan Swamp forest below the pond dam. It winds its way almost due south across the freshwater swamp to the Chowan River. Many of the wildlife species native to this part of the state can be found along the trail, among them bear, bobcats, and deer.

Topo Maps: Winton, Beckford

Counties: Gates, Chowan

(1) Gates County Rt. 1400 bridge to NC 37 bridge on the outskirts of Gatesville

Drop: 2′	**Time:** 4 hrs.
Difficulty: A	**Scenery:** A
Distance: 5.3 mi.	**Water Quality:** Good

Gauge: None. Runnable year round except following long dry spells when one may have to do a little wading through the first mile or so.

Difficulties: Downed trees. The trail is maintained by volunteers, so any help from their friends--namely you--will be appreciated. Please do not use chopping tools.

For those who wish to enter the creek from the pond, an easy carry over Rt. 1400 can be made.

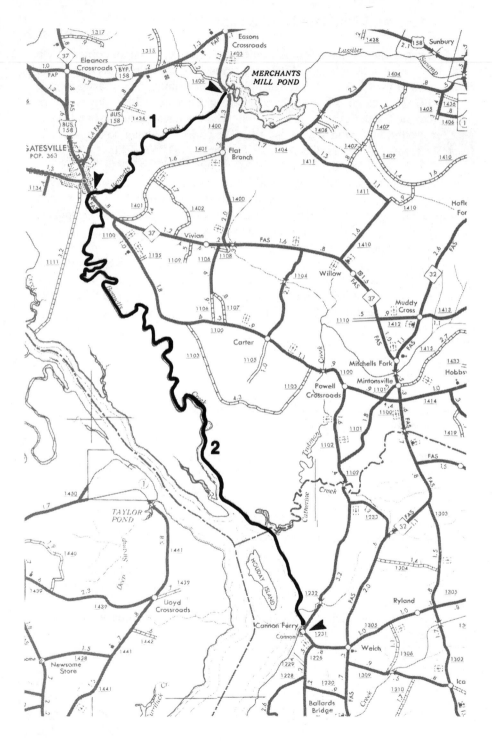

Merchants Mill Pond

(2) NC 37 bridge to wildlife access area at Cannon Ferry on the Chowan River and at the end of Chowan County Rts. 1232 and 1231

Drop: 0′	**Time:** 8-12 hrs.
Difficulty: A	**Scenery:** A
Distance: 14.9 mi.	**Water Quality:** Good

Gauge: None. Runnable year round.

Difficulties: Bennetts Creek winds broad and flat on its way to the Chowan. Through most of the 15-mile distance the water and forests merge without a clear boundary. Thus, except for a small hillock of privately owned high ground about ten miles down on the left bank and the primitive campsite at Hermit Island, it is quite difficult to step out of the canoe to lunch, stretch, or relieve oneself. The final two and a half to three miles are along the broad Chowan, where wind, waves, or a sudden thunderstorm will be a serious problem for a canoe. Allow a full day to make a leisurely trip. Be prepared with appropriate clothing, food, and emergency gear, and check the weather forecast before leaving.

Appendix

The following groups located primarily in the Piedmont and Coastal Plains are organized around their interest in local rivers and streams. You may be assured that they will accept and appreciate your support.

Cape Fear River Assembly
P.O. Box 1089
Fayetteville, NC 28302

Catawba River Foundation, Inc.
926 Elizabeth Avenue, Suite 403-A
Charlotte, NC 28204

Clean Water Fund of North Carolina
29½ Page Avenue
Asheville, NC 28801

Dan River Canoe Trail Club
P.O. Box 1375
Danville, NC 24543

Eno River Association
4419 Guess Road
Durham, NC 27712

Friends of the Uwharrie
1317 Allred Street
Asheboro, NC 28203

Haw River Assembly
P.O. Box 187
Bynum, NC 27228

Izaak Walton League
White Oak River Chapter
c/o Al Fox
126 Sutton Drive
Cape Carteret, NC 28584

Lumber River Basin Committee
P.O. Box 2185
Lumberton, NC 28359

Lumber River Conservancy
P.O. Box 1889
Lumberton, NC 28359

Neuse River Foundation
P.O. Box 15451
New Bern, NC 28560

Neuse–White Oak Advisory Committee
7010 Thunder Mountain Road
Efland, NC 27243-9772

North Carolina Stream Watch
DENR Division of Water Resources
1611 Mail Service Center
Raleigh, NC 27699-1611

Pamlico–Tar River Foundation
109 Gladden Street
Washingon, NC 27889

Protect Our Water
1509 Smith Level Road
Chapel Hill, NC 27516

RiverLink
P.O. Box 15488
Asheville, NC 28813-0488

Save Our Rivers
P.O. Box 122
Franklin, NC 28744

Yadkin-Pee Dee River Lakes Project
P.O. Box 338
Badin, NC 28009

Stream Index